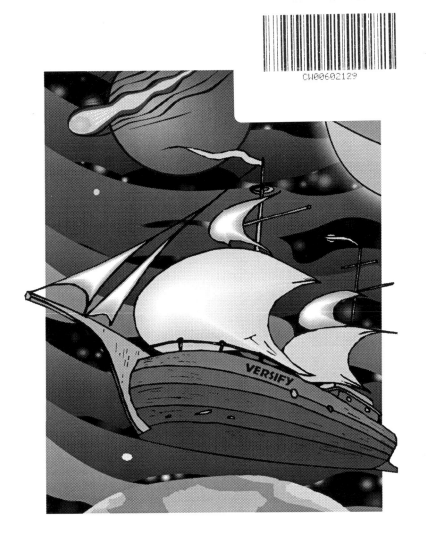

VERSIFY

POETIC VOYAGES YORK

Edited by Allison Dowse

First published in Great Britain in 2001 by
YOUNG WRITERS
Remus House,
Coltsfoot Drive,
Peterborough, PE2 9JX
Telephone (01733) 890066

HB ISBN 0 75433 210 1
SB ISBN 0 75433 211 X

FOREWORD

Young Writers was established in 1991 with the aim to promote creative writing in children, to make reading and writing poetry fun.

This year once again, proved to be a tremendous success with over 88,000 entries received nationwide.

The Poetic Voyages competition has shown us the high standard of work and effort that children are capable of today. It is a reflection of the teaching skills in schools, the enthusiasm and creativity they have injected into their pupils shines clearly within this anthology.

The task of selecting poems was therefore a difficult one but nevertheless, an enjoyable experience. We hope you are as pleased with the final selection in *Poetic Voyages York* as we are.

CONTENTS

Joshua Dawson	16
Joel Taylor	17
Charlotte Angove	17
Emily Christy	18
Tanya Scarr	18
Emma Brown	19
Helina Farah	19
Emma Weston	20
Matthew Hields	20
Antonia Bailey	21
Laura Brookshaw	21
Rebecca Kelly	22
Thomas Whitaker	22
Spencer Brown	22
Christie Lilburn	23
Amy Green	23
Heather Stead	23
Joseph Crockett	24
Darren Henderson	24
Alistair Dobson	24
Ben Dalton-Riggs	25
Robert Walden	25
Joe Embleton	25
Rhys Savage	26
Ashleigh Robinson	26
Sam Pugh	27
Amy Poole	27
Joe Blackmore	28
Zoey Williams	28
Hannah Moate	28
Laura Witham	29
Natalie Hodgson	29
Rebecca Wilson	29
Martyn Allison	30
Arran Woodford	30
Chlöe Girvan	31
Rachel Sawyer	31
Sarah Wharton	32

Fishergate CP School

James Lawrance   81
Bridie Doy   82

Osbaldwick Primary School
            Aimee Pearcy   82
            Jason Hollis   83
            Chloe Jones   83
            Rachael Umpleby   84
            Sophie Winship   84
            Claire Morley   85
            Rebecca Ward   86

St George's RC School
            Nicola Bradshaw   87
            Thomas Khan   87
            Ieuan Solanki   87
            Stephanie Ireland 88
            Charlotte Holmes 88
            Megan Simpson   88
            Chantelle Burn   89
            Lauren Lea Husband 89
            Charlotte Ellis   89
            Rachael Anderson 90
            Maddy Burrows   90

St Olave's School
            Jonathan Bairstow   91
            Sylvia Lai Mun Wong 91
            Sebastian Bachelor   92
            Hannah Gilford   92
            Dominic Hanly   93
            Tom Scott   93
            Ben Eaves   94
            Alexander Lee   94
            Alastair Penty   95
            Callum Stark   96
            Ben Naughton   96
            Andrew Doyle   97

Edward Mackenzie	97
Edmund Pang	98
Megan Hall	98
Alice Jacobs	99
Louise Walters	99
Oliver Hawking	100
Anna Peach	100
Joy Barker	101
Jack Page	101
Amelia Smalley	102

Slingsby CP School

Christopher Dean	102
Becky Swallow	103
Lucy Harrison	103
Joshua Clarke	104
Emma Jane Hatfield	104
Lynsey Hatfield	104
Rebecca Dring	105
Charles Morfoot	105
Natasha Pearse	105
Carrie-Anne Wallace	106
James Baker	106

Stamford Bridge Primary School

Danny Burke	107
Liam Archer	107
Chloé Evans	108
George Dalby	109
Emma Green	110
Roxanne Oldfield	111
Sarah McLeod	112
Thomas Smithson	112
Rosie Burke	113
Jonathan Andrew	114
Sam Dalby	114
Lauren Cameron	115
Jack Winfield	115

Michael Ward	139
Hannah Crowley	140
Lucy Glew	140
Jack Bond	141
Charles Armstrong	142
Philip Main	142
Olivia Alderson-Tuck	143
Matthew Fennell	144
Adam Green	144
Emma Doughty	145
Charlotte Helme	146
Ashley Patel	147
Laura Hammond	148
James Ross	148
Craig Benn	149
George Leadley	150

Welburn CP School

Ben Wynne	150
Bethany Tildesley	151
Amy Louise Batty	152
Nick Riley	152
Natalie Skirrow	153
Faith Somers	154
Nicholas Corbett	154
Jessica Townley	155
Ben Cohen	155
Katy Matthews	156
Christopher Thorp	156
Matthew Shaw	157
Lucy Holmes	158
Ben Daniels	159

The Poems

FOOTY FANS

Liverpool fans, already there watching the match, not a care.
Man U fans there's a goal, cover your ears it was Andy Cole.
Arsenal fans, wearing red, one with a little hat on his head.
Sunderland fans, what a crowd, that'll make the players proud.
Man C fans, big aren't they, they'll probably stay only till May.
Leeds fans, coming down, the toughest group in town.
Ipswich fans, a roar from them, dressed in blue to the hem.
Leicester fans, cheering on their team, their shouts are like a
                       massive sound beam.
Chelsea fans, very blue, every time there's a match they
                       come down with flu.
Aston Villa fans, dressed to the nines, the grown-ups
                       drinking alcoholic wines.
Bradford fans, having a laugh, blocking off the stands path.
Southampton fans, with mobile phones cheering with very loud tones.
Middlesborough fans, drinking beer, leaning over the stands, not a fear.
Everton fans, they're really strong, they won't do anything wrong.
Charlton fans, loads of goals, they'll strap themselves to the posts and
                       stay there till they turn into ghosts.
Sheffield fans, do anything to be loyal that they turn very royal.
York fans, don't need to travel, for the stadium is nearly on their gravel.
Birmingham fans, always late, they'll have to put beer out for bait.

Footy fans full with joy except when they lose they're full with annoy.

Jonathon Doubtfire (10)
Barmby Moor CE Primary School

No Wonder

No wonder he looks really old
No wonder he is grey
And can not hear
Or jump,
Or catch,
Or even run away.
No wonder that he sleeps all day
No wonder he is fat
And only dreams of catching things
And chasing neighbour's cats!

So fight your fights
In dog-dream night
Deep within your bed . . .

Today's your day
And we all say . . .

Happy Birthday Fred!

Katie Cowley (10)
Barmby Moor CE Primary School

My Cat

My cat is as black as shiny coal,
White like paper,
White like slushy snow.
Her miaow as soft as a mouse's squeak
Her hiss is like a snake
Her paws as soft as silk.

Ben Richardson (10)
Barmby Moor CE Primary School

KENNING'S BUNNY

Ear-twitcher,
Teeth-clicker,
Carrot-muncher,
Always-cruncher,
Mad-hopper,
Grass-chopper,
Cute-cuddler,
Not a muddler,
Loud-stamper,
Quite a scamper,
Fast-runner,
A big stunner.

Clare Perkins (9)
Barmby Moor CE Primary School

OUR DOLPHIN

Grey like the shimmering ocean,
Eyes like starry sapphires,
Fins like dripping razors,
Giggles like a laughing hyena,
I will feed it with glowing fish,
Teach it many tricks,
I will dance with it, prance with it
Till the sun has set.
And in the morning in the dusk
I shall stroke it smooth.

Katie Rose (11)
Barmby Moor CE Primary School

OUR SHARK

Our shark is a deadly maneater
Lurking through the murky sea,
Teeth like sharp razors dripping with red blood,
Fins like drenched blades,
Eyes as red as small rubies,
His tail is like a wagging arrow
His body is like a sinking moon,
We shall feed him with golden fish.

Abigail Fisher & Kirstie Roberts (10)
Barmby Moor CE Primary School

A VICTIM OF A NIGHTMARE

It's alright
Oh no it's not.
The adrenaline rush
Tearing through my
Lava like blood.
A dream gone terribly wrong
Dark, everything is dark.
I want to cry
It won't let me.
The power of heat
Burning my vocal chords
A burning spike ball
Tearing my brain to pieces.

I am a victim of a nightmare!

Stuart Lunn (10)
Clifton Without Junior School

THE ESCAPE

The cat stood there brave and tall
With all the scratch marks against the wall.
The mouse stood shaking, his eyes a-blazing,
He was cornered.

The cat hissed like a snake,
Waiting to pounce on its prey.
The victim darted through the predator's legs.

The chase began!

The mouse was sprinting through the kitchen, heart pounding
Over dirty dishes, under tall tables, and at last through
                                    the dingy doorway.

Suddenly, the cat's paws appeared in front of the mind-boggled mouse.
But that didn't stop him!

Terrified, the mouse dodged the cat's giant claws,
The mouse took a final breath and leapt to freedom.

Joseph Whiting, Victoria Needham, Shannon O'Malley,
Joe Cooper, Anthony Evans (11) & Gemma Lockey (10)
Clifton Without Junior School

TRAVELLING

U FOs are exciting
F lying in the air
O h I would love to travel in a UFO.

C ars coming and going
A nd I travel by
R acing passed I go.

Naim Mohammed (8)
Clifton Without Junior School

GERMAN JEWS HAVE RAGGED OLD CLOTHES

German Jews have ragged old clothes and no shoes or socks,
They're very cold in a tiny room.
People give them food, but very cold food,
And give them no showers at all.
They never get anything warm, just cold things,
In a cold room with no fresh air.
The Jews are squashed in the tiny room,
Because there are six people in one tiny room.
They have not one single toilet,
They are very sad.
Everything is gone they get only cold things
And no showers or toilets or nice clothes or shoes and socks.

Rachel Hopwood (10)
Clifton Without Junior School

FEAR

Fear!
My heart, it's racing full speed
The pain is burning inside me
My lips are trembling, my teeth are clenching!
It's such a nightmare fear.
Fear!
My fingers have frozen, my horror carries on
My terror will never stop, go away fear!
Just go away! It's such a nightmare fear.

Laura Pilmoor (11)
Clifton Without Junior School

DEPRESSION

They took our rights and family
They blamed it on us.
We travelled like cattle for days on trains
The room we slept in was grey and dull,
They said we could have a shower
But no, it was gas.
We dug our own graves,
We stand before them
Dead.
Some dying of diseases
Some dying of hunger
But some die of depression.

Hayley Wilkinson (11)
Clifton Without Junior School

IT'S A NIGHTMARE WORLD

Fear!
Run, run away
Run far away
Never come back.
Feel the goosebumps,
Feel the cold,
Hear the things that go bump in the night
Feel the evil in you
It's a nightmare world.

Blaine Atkinson (11)
Clifton Without Junior School

HOLLAND

H   olland is a popular place
O   ut of all my favourite places, Holland is at the top of my list,
L   ovely flowers stand out in the sun.
L   ovely land, buildings and nature
A   ll the animals have their own piece of land
N   ot many people hate Holland.
D   ogs and cats and other animals are looked after properly.

Rebecca Benson (7)
Clifton Without Junior School

TUNISIA

Sunny, relaxing pools
Sandy, sunny beaches
Lovely, relaxing shops
See the historic cities of Tunisia.
They will make you happy to see,
Or why don't you go swimming in the sea?

Martin Ingle (11)
Clifton Without Junior School

PALM TREE POEM

Relax on the lovely beach
Heathrow Airport will put it in reach
Dance at the exciting disco,
Swim in the fun pool,
And your holiday will be cool.

David Friend (10)
Clifton Without Junior School

HUNG

Running down the street hurting the bottom of your feet
Been whipped by eleven men with eleven stripes each,
Now you jump, just out of reach, it feels like you're in purgatory,
Isn't this a tragedy, it is, isn't this a tragedy?

I was caught, I was hung, I felt like I was dead,
When I now nearly lost my head.
They filled the room up with gas and just
Now I started to pass, I went.

Nathan Potter (10)
Clifton Without Junior School

TERROR

Terror
Alone in a house
Down in the cellar
Tears hot and sweaty
Clothes sticking
Wake up in the middle of the night
Hear a wolf howling
Getting goosebumps
Nails screeching down the blackboard
Stiff like a statue
Blood rushing down your veins
Trembling with fear
Shaking in your shoes.

Jordan Ness (10)
Clifton Without Junior School

THE FEAR

Horror!

The heart of darkness.

The freezing cold horror
Cutting and scratching
Trying to get it out of my head
My brain is rolling.
It is like a nightmare world.
The happiness in your heart fades!
It goes black.

Goosebumps under my skin.
The pain has gone, there is nothing within.

Lorna Howard (10)
Clifton Without Junior School

HORROR

The sweat trickling down your face
Just standing there
Like a rock
Feeling numb.
A thousand daggers are in your back
You are trying to look through a window,
But you can't see anything.
Having your soul ripped out of your body
You are hearing people screaming, crying, shouting.

This is fear.

Luke Dunford (11)
Clifton Without Junior School

HORROR

Horror!
The sweat was running down my face,
I started to shake
Then I heard it,
My heart, pumping blood up to my head
Then everything was blurred,
I heard it again
It was as if I were a block of ice
Then my eyes widened
I just stood there staring
Then I saw a shadow
It was him!

Laura Wiseman (10)
Clifton Without Junior School

TERROR

Terror
Knots tying
Goosebumps prickling
Body shaking
Blood thumping
Throat clogging
Adrenaline bursting
I am screaming
Terror.

Natasha Francksen (10)
Clifton Without Junior School

HORROR

Fear,
The nightmare world of fear.
Panic,
The sweat of panic.
Horror,
Your mouth opens wide like a black hole.
Terror,
The heart of darkness.

The animal of fear,
Haunting everyone it sees,
Big, black, bold eyes,
The animal of fear, you never know where it is.

The ghost of panic,
It always makes you scream,
It makes you sweat,
It makes you rip your hair out.

The black hole of horror,
Pulls in everything it sees,
It never lets you go,
Like being wrapped in old, bloodstained chains.

Terror . . .

Joe Cooper (11)
Clifton Without Junior School

ITALIA

Discos at night,
And cafés at day,
The cobbled streets are very ornate,
We hope you have fun at this extravagant lake.

With the tropical pools,
You will be able to cool,
And stylish shops,
You can shop 'til you drop.

Jasmine McNeill (10)
Clifton Without Junior School

HORROR

The horror of the darkness
It's an endless nightmare
The sweat on your forehead
The fear of dying
You freeze in pain
The heart of terror taking you away into your fear.

The heart of darkness
The pain within.

Richard Robson (11)
Clifton Without Junior School

HEART OF EVIL

Horror!
Evil needles stabbing in my eyes.
Fear!
Cold shivers down my spine.
Panic!
Widened eyes of shock.
Terror!
Screaming noises.
The tragic death of calm.

Melanie Benfield (11)
Clifton Without Junior School

FEAR OUTSIDE

The fear was deep beneath me,
Within me.
I hid, hid from the killer.
I couldn't speak,
I couldn't move,
My heart was ringing, pounding fast
My breath was seen in the air
A cloud of mist
I shook, shook and rattled the bushes
Footsteps came nearer and nearer
Closer and closer.
I didn't dare move, I ran, ran fast to the end
The first post
Death was near, death was happening,
The fear outside.

Mae Woodcock (10)
Clifton Without Junior School

PARIS

It was in Paris
At the top of the Eiffel Tower
That I couldn't see very far
On a hot, hazy day.

We went to the biggest swimming pool,
It had really big, big slides
And they were very, very fast!

Sophie Glasby (8)
Clifton Without Junior School

14

NIGHTMARE WORLD

Goosebumps, you can see your breath,
You're so cold and terrified you can't move,
You're stiff as a bone,
You start to shake you try to stop but you can't
You're feeling like you need to run - you need to get out of here
You think you hear a noise but you realise it is your imagination,
You get a big lump in the back of your throat
You're swallowing all the time,
You sweat and then you can't take it any more, you run.

The horror!

Kelly Hodges (10)
Clifton Without Junior School

THE CARIBBEAN

The Caribbean is the ideal place for you
Water skiing, scuba diving, windsurfing too
A king-size bed, a hairdryer, a telephone,
A four-poster bed, in-room bar and plush bathrobes.

Golf and country clubs will make you want to dash -
You'll end up spending nearly all your cash!
A European spa will make you run,
Sailing, water parks, lots and lots of fun,

Thinking of it makes me want to spend,
But we'll like it and like it until the very end!

Nathan Gascon-Saiz (10)
Clifton Without Junior School

FEAR

Fear!
Screaming,
Stabbing,
You tear your house apart,
The heart of darkness is coming closer,
Death!
Horror,
Panic,
Your world is falling to pieces,
Your body is frozen,
A thousand pins and nails stabbing in your body,
You can't get away,
Evil is right in front of you,
Staring you in the eye,
You never wake up from your nightmare.

Gina Murphy (11)
Clifton Without Junior School

TERROR

Breathing
Short, sharp breaths.
Body, legs and arms turn to jelly,
Weak and strengthless.
I wait.

The spirits are free, they're pulling out souls.
I wait.

Joshua Dawson (10)
Clifton Without Junior School

THE SUN

The sun is a giant fireball callous to the planets around.

A conflagration that will deteriorate through time.

A basketball in the sky
A blaze from the Earth.

The sun is a blazing light bulb
Shining on full power.

A drop of water seeping through a crack.

The light of the galaxy
Fire of man.

Joel Taylor (10)
Clifton Without Junior School

MY NANNY'S HOUSE

My nanny's so cuddly
I'm glad that she's here
She gives a lot of things to me
My mum even nags my nanny,
To stop giving me things.

My grandad is full of tricks and jokes
Up his sleeve
He's got so many puppets,
I don't know how many!

Charlotte Angove (7)
Clifton Without Junior School

SUN

The sun is an illuminous ball of fire
It shines whenever it does not rain
It is a fluorescent massive torch.

It seems like a ginormous ball of gas,
That shimmers like sausages.
When it is sunny it smiles down on you
But when it rains it's a ball of thunder.

It sounds like timid echoes
Especially in the sunlit sky
There is more entrance into the day,
In the summer space,
Lots of conscious clouds focus on the smiley sun
On the brightest day of the year.

It looks like baked buns in a cooker overnight
But then dawn returns and it starts to rise
The sun is a ball shining on our planet.

Emily Christy (9)
Clifton Without Junior School

GUESS WHAT?

Sleeping on the bed,
Resting its little head,
Doesn't make a sound,
When nobody's around,
Waking up to a cuddle,
In the middle of a huddle,
Gives itself a lick,
Then goes to see the chick!

Tanya Scarr (10)
Clifton Without Junior School

THE SUN

The sun is an immense gold coin, owned by the King of gods,
It is a strip of lightning flashing along a road of darkness,
It's a splosh of paint,
Leader of the planets
And when clouds pass by, everything is still and misty.

The sun is an exotic planet made only of sand,
It is beautiful locks of golden hair swayed by a child,
It has warm colours,
A cheery face,
Humongous ball of fire, always ready to shine down on us.

Emma Brown (9)
Clifton Without Junior School

THE MOON

The moon is a silver candle in the sky
It is a bright, glowing crystal in the ocean
The moon is white and glittering
The moon is a silver candle in the sky.

The moon is a silver candle in the sky
It is a big, white sphere skimming across the sky
It is like a big, white Tipp-Ex splash on black paper
The moon is a silver candle in the sky.

The moon is a silver candle in the sky
It is a vast snowflake lit up by the sun
It is a golden cloud dancing in the darkness
The moon is a silver candle in the sky.

Helina Farah (10)
Clifton Without Junior School

THE MOON

The moon is like a shiny bowling ball
It is beautiful, bright, big and bold
It is like a twinkle and sparkles like frost
It looks scary and cold.

The moon is shiny but when clouds
Go past it looks like horrible
Black bits being scrunched up.
It is sparkly eyes staring,
It is a knife of light piercing
Through the darkness,
It is like a round face glaring.

Emma Weston (10)
Clifton Without Junior School

SUN

The sun is a ball of the heavens
It is a rolling spirit device
Key of the God and Heaven
Great keeper of space
It is a ball of fantasy
The goddess of science
Master of the flame
The dawn of life
The sun's a spirit's home
A truly glorious sight
The spirit of day shall glow
Away as long as Earth shall live.

Matthew Hields (10)
Clifton Without Junior School

SPACESHIP

S ome aliens once came down to Earth, in a rocketship
P arents or children couldn't move either of their lips
A n alien came up and shook my hand,
C all the alien's band!
E veryone hated them.
S paceship was about to go,
H e didn't like Earth much.
I didn't want the aliens to go,
P eople did though!

Antonia Bailey (8)
Clifton Without Junior School

LIFE'S AN ADVENTURE!

A ll I do is travel,
D riving vans and trains,
V oyages waiting out there for me,
E xtraordinary! Trucks and cranes
N o one's here to stop me,
T anks, boats and ferries
U nicorns,
R un! They're no friends of Terry's!
E veryone come, enjoy the ride.

Laura Brookshaw (8)
Clifton Without Junior School

SEASIDE

S   easide sun awaits us
E   xcited faces on the beach
A   n ice cream shop makes ice cream
S   wishing seas make the sand wet
I   think I should live at the sea
D   eep seas are near
E   veryone is happy.

Rebecca Kelly (9)
Clifton Without Junior School

MERCURY

M   en on Mercury
E   veryone can go,
R   esting in a crater,
C   o-ops and shops of the future,
U   FOs flying around,
R   ound the world in a week,
Y   ou all own a spaceship.

Thomas Whitaker (8)
Clifton Without Junior School

FRANCE

F   ood for animals is low,
R   ain is starting to come,
A   nimals are happy because they can hibernate,
N   ow it is winter children won't be playing out,
C   old weather is upon us,
E   veryone is putting warm clothes on.

Spencer Brown (7)
Clifton Without Junior School

INDIA

I ndia can be very hot and rainy
N aughty children and people there play jokes and games for a laugh
and for celebrations
D elightful food hot or cold, there's lots of tasty things and drinks too
I slands there are lovely places to go when it's hot and sunny
A nd I haven't forgotten about this word it all spells India!

Christie Lilburn (8)
Clifton Without Junior School

INDIA

I n India you can get lots of different animals to England
N aughty people play jokes on people on a celebration
D elightful people live in India
I ndia is a very nice place to look around
A nd India is a very nice place to live.

Amy Green (9)
Clifton Without Junior School

OASIS

O asis is fun,
A ll the sports, shopping and swimming
S wimming is fun, down all the slides
I n and out of huts
S nuggle down until another day!

Heather Stead (7)
Clifton Without Junior School

THE MOON

The moon is a belt of light leaving darkness behind
A silver spirit of night-time wonders seeking countries all around
A ghostly spirit in the sparkling sky,
A dagger slicing through the blackness as though it's water,
It's as quiet as a mouse,
It's as light as fire,
Still very much like a statue.

Joseph Crockett (9)
Clifton Without Junior School

THE MOON

The moon is a mysterious white ball
That guides the way through the galaxy
Thunder slices away anything among its tracks.

The moon is a blank football slithering around in the dark
Heaven is fire, Hell is sad,
Light is a candle of the galaxy, darkness blows it out.

Darren Henderson (9)
Clifton Without Junior School

THE MOON

The moon is a planet of light moving across the night sky
A silver blade cutting through our solar system.
A mysterious ball seeking the world
The moon is a ghostly galleon sailing across the sky
The moon is a ray of grey light in the night
A scoop of cheese lighting up the midnight sky.

Alistair Dobson (10)
Clifton Without Junior School

THE WONDROUS STARS

The stars are golden wonders high up in the sky
The stars are little tears from a baby's cry.
And yet the stars are dragonflies high up in the sky
They watch us all from Heaven as day and night go by.
Oh yes the stars are wondrous things but still
I wonder why
Of all the years I've been here they never come down from the sky?

Ben Dalton-Riggs (9)
Clifton Without Junior School

STARS

The sparkly stars shoot past the dull, dingy, dark Earth
And then the night falls, but soon the stars come out,
Then lights the night with its bright, astonishing light
Stars are bright that also light up the dark Earth at night
There are small lights piercing through the dingy, dark
                                      surface of the globe
Space is filled with small, twinkling stars.

Robert Walden (9)
Clifton Without Junior School

MOON

The moon is a gigantic silvery sphere shining in the midnight sky
Like a candle seeking in the sky.
It's as spooky as a sword of light
Slicing through the darkness.
A gigantic black sky
Surrounding a white football.

Joe Embleton (10)
Clifton Without Junior School

SUN

The sun is a fiery ball piercing the darkness
A planet of light rolling across the sky
Blazing ball
A golden plate.

A golden ball lighting up the emptiness of Earth.
The great being pulled across the sky
Silvery ball of light
Brightening up the world.

The sun is a shield blocking all darkness
From getting to the world
A ball of light shooting across the sky.

A torch shining
Spirit of the world.

Rhys Savage (9)
Clifton Without Junior School

HIGHWAYMAN'S HORSE

The highwayman's horse is as powerful as a speeding rocket
It's as graceful as a swan
Hooves as shiny as gold,
A coat of silky skin
It is as swift as an eagle in flight
As it's galloping, galloping, galloping.

As black as the dark night
Its mane sparkles in the moonlight.

It is as wild as a lion catching its prey.

Ashleigh Robinson (10)
Clifton Without Junior School

MOON, OH LIGHT MOON

The moon is a screwed up piece of paper flicked across the sky
Like a mysterious ball guarding the castle of reflection.

A white glowing ball of spirit trapping all the darkness
The football trophy leading to the hall of fame
A key opening the door to light.

An enormous light in a big, black attic,
The new bright life
Goddess of light making a shining ball in the bright midnight sky
Leaving the darkness behind him.

Sam Pugh (10)
Clifton Without Junior School

THE HIGHWAYMAN'S HORSE

The highwayman's horse is a shield of life,
It can be as silent as the night.
The highwayman's horse is as powerful
As a missile and as wild as a bronco,
It is a ghostly stallion as great as a galleon.
The highwayman's horse is the spirit of the night,
And keeper of the inner light.
It is a shadowy strength waiting to be unleashed.
The highwayman's horse is the guardian of life.

Amy Poole (9)
Clifton Without Junior School

THE MOON

The moon is a mysterious white ball
Skimming across the sky
The moon is a scary spirit
It lights up the dark sky
It is a white sphere in the sky
It looks like a ghostly galleon
It lights up the dark sky like a massive round torch.

Jack Blackmore (10)
Clifton Without Junior School

THE MOON

The moon is a guiding light
Leading the passage to the moon,
Spooky like a torch in the sky
It's a sword light piercing through the darkness,
And a shield of light darkness behind.
A ball of light slowly fighting
Through the darkness.

Zoey Williams (10)
Clifton Without Junior School

NAME THE ANIMALS

They flip their flippers up and down,
Their necks are really long,
They waddle and widdle,
They prowl and growl,
And bark at everyone.

Hannah Moate (10)
Clifton Without Junior School

EXCITING HOLIDAYS

H appy people walking around,
O n the beach the sun is shining,
L ying near the pool
I ce creams melting in the sun,
D odging on the dodgems,
A musing places to go and see,
Y ucky sea water in your mouth, quick spit it out!

Laura Witham (9)
Clifton Without Junior School

SADNESS

Sadness is blue,
It smells like the sea,
It tastes like a tear,
Sadness sounds like a dolphin,
It feels thin and soft,
Sadness lives in a cold, dark cave.

Natalie Hodgson (9)
Clifton Without Junior School

WHAT IS IT?

A nose twitcher,
A carrot eater,
A large hopper,
A cuddle lover,
A sweet sleeper,
A cute looker,
A naughty nibbler.

Rebecca Wilson (10)
Clifton Without Junior School

WEATHER

Rain, rain you're such a pain
I hate you a lot
I don't get to play with my mates
Rain, rain you're such a pain.

Snow, snow you're very cold
But I can mould you into a snowman
Which covers me so I can make my play
Snow, snow you're very cold.

Sun, sun you're so much fun
You help us get our work done
So we can have some fun
Sun, sun you're so much fun.

Martyn Allison (11)
Clifton Without Junior School

THE MOON

The moon is a planet of light
Moving across the night sky
A silver blade cutting through
Our solar system.
A mysterious ball
Seeking the world
The moon is a ghostly galleon sailing
Across the sky.
The moon is a ray of grey light in the night.
A scoop of cheese lighting up the midnight sky.

Arran Woodford (9)
Clifton Without Junior School

LOOKING UP TO HEAVEN

Once there was a minute meadow,
And in the middle looking up was Heaven.

I looked up to Heaven and saw
My sister and I galloping on polo ponies.

My granny looked up to Heaven,
And saw me knocking on her door.

I looked up to Heaven,
And saw my dad with all his bills paid.

A teacher looked up to Heaven
And saw a box full of smiles to give to her well behaved class.

I looked up to Heaven and saw
Ali G coming to York in his respected car.

My mum looked up to Heaven . . .

Chlöe Girvan (10)
Clifton Without Junior School

THE MOON

The moon is like . . . a glowing disco ball lighting up the night,
A torch in the dark cupboard,
A slice of lemon thrown into space,
An enormous creamy sphere
Floating in the atmosphere,
A scoop of butter placed onto a black plate,
A bright light,
The moon is . . . the spirit of the night.

Rachel Sawyer (9)
Clifton Without Junior School

WITCHES

Cackling round the pot
Thinking up a plot
Flying out on brooms
They have horrible scary rooms
With warts on their face
They think children are a disgrace
So bringing it all together
I hate witches!

Sarah Wharton (11)
Clifton Without Junior School

WHAT AM I?

I am spiky
And come out at night
I hibernate
And curl up in a ball very tight
There are a lot who get squashed but not me
And we sometimes live in the bottom of a tree.

Lucy Botterill (9)
Clifton Without Junior School

THE BULL FROM HULL

There was an extremely large bull
Who sat in the middle of Hull
For he said 'Help me Lord
I'm exceedingly bored
And it looks like my life is dull'.

Matthew Atlay (11)
Clifton Without Junior School

SEAWORLD

It was at Seaworld
I saw my Aunty Jackie
We had so much fun.

It was at Seaworld
I pushed my dad in the pool
He made a big *splash!*

Emma Wilson (8)
Clifton Without Junior School

FLORIDA!

It was in Florida
I was in a swimming pool
With Lorna.

It was in Florida
I saw Mickey Mouse
He was cute!

Bryony Herbert (8)
Clifton Without Junior School

THE MOON IS . . .

The moon is a shining star
In the moonlight seeking through the fields.
The moon is a spotty sphere
Circling the Earth.
It is a strange-looking planet.

Tom Muller (9)
Clifton Without Junior School

MARS

Mars is a burning ball with heat very high.
Mars is a red ball rotating at one hundred miles an hour.
Mars is a bonfire burning in the sky furiously.
Mars is a red sweater floating high above the blue sky.
Mars is a red Mini on its side.
Mars is a red noticeboard except astronauts look at it, not the public.
Mars is a red pencil case spinning at different angles.
Mars is a racing dog with a red tabard racing at a thousand light years.

Lewis Ashton (9)
Clifton Without Junior School

HAPPINESS

Happiness is yellow,
It smells like daisies.
Happiness tastes like bananas.
Happiness sounds like the fresh breeze,
It feels like Playdoh.
Happiness lives high in the hills.

Hayley Bushell (9)
Clifton Without Junior School

HOPE

Hope is yellow,
It smells like chocolate ice cream.
Hope tastes like sweets and chocolate
It sounds like sweet songs,
It feels soft and tender.
Hope lives in the hearts of good people.

Zoe Smith (9)
Clifton Without Junior School

CHOCOLATE

Chocolate is like Heaven itself.
Chocolate is like a brown tree.
Chocolate is as sweet as a strawberry.

Chocolate is like brown silk.
Chocolate is like gold.
Chocolate is like a smooth powder.

Joe Fox (8)
Clifton Without Junior School

THE STREAM RUNNING PAST

The stream running past
Through the lovely bank
With seagulls swooping past
The bank looks as blue as the bright sky
The people who walk past the bank
The breeze brushes their cheeks.

Daniel Zambelli (10)
Clifton Without Junior School

SADNESS

Sadness is blue,
It smells like the sea,
It tastes like a tear.
Sadness sounds like a mermaid's song,
It feels thin and silky.
Sadness lives in a lake.

Jazmine Linklater (8)
Clifton Without Junior School

THE BRIGHT SUN

The sun is a bright lazy ball.
It is a giant football.
It's a dinosaur that breathes fire.
It is like a brand new bulb that has just been made.
It is as big as the Earth.
It has a shiny model right in the middle.
There is a giant's head in the sky that stands out.
It's an enormous sun lolly.
It looks like a bright orange bun.
It's a glass of light.

Gemma Rutt (9)
Clifton Without Junior School

SEASONS

Summer,
Glittering sun,
Making huge sand castles,
Splashing about in the ocean,
Blue skies.

Autumn,
Dry leaves falling,
Dancing flames in dark skies,
Chilly nights assault us again,
Winds howl.

Ruth Brandon (10)
Clifton Without Junior School

THERE'S A SPIDER IN MY BED

There's a spider in my bed,
There's a spider in my bed
With its creepy-crawly
Spiky, scrawny, spidery legs.

I don't know where it came from
I don't really care,
All I know is,
I don't want it there!

I hate the hairs
On its huge, fat tummy.
So then I cried,
'Mummy, Mummy!'

I also hate its long, hairy legs,
And huge, goggly eyes.
So I just went to swat it
And I prayed that it died.
And it did!

Hannah Markham (10)
Clifton Without Junior School

DEATH TRAP

He's being chased by a man with a 2X4,
He's cornered by evil in a dark alley.
There's shadows in the window,
He's alone in the house,
He's got goosebumps on his arms,
He's dead!

In a nightmare world.

Michael Lee (10)
Clifton Without Junior School

PEACE

There once was an ornate mirror,
Tucked away in a basement.

One day a baby looked through the mirror
And saw her life ahead of her.

One day a teacher peered through the window
And saw a happy smiling class.

One day an old lady looked into a misty window
And saw a cure for her illness.

On a quiet, sunny day Jesus glanced into the window
And saw happiness and no enemies.

One day a fish stared into the mirror
And saw no pollution.

One frosty day a dog gaped through the mirror
And saw a huge bone.

One snowy day a postman peered into the mirror
And saw no post.

Samantha Robertson (11)
Clifton Without Junior School

SADNESS

Sadness is purple,
It smells like burnt toast.
Sadness tastes like eggs bubbling,
It sounds like water coming from the tap,
It feels like spoons banging together.
Sadness lives in a mucky mountain.

Kelly Brigham (9)
Clifton Without Junior School

THE DEVIL

There was once an evil devil,
Hidden away in the corner of a room.

One evening a top footballer looked into the devil's eyes
And saw himself being transferred to a Sunday league team.

A singer looked into the devil's eyes
And saw herself falling off the stage.

A cat peeped into the devil's eyes
And saw a big, angry dog.

A paper boy stared into the devil's eyes
And saw his bike being thrown into the river.

A devil looked into his own eyes
And saw world peace.

A hippie peered into the devil's eyes
And saw World War III.

God and Jesus looked into the devil's eyes together
And the devil's eyes popped out!

James Heslop (11)
Clifton Without Junior School

LOVE

Love is red,
It smells like strawberries.
Love tastes like a piece of birthday cake,
It sounds like trickling water,
It feels like a heart pumping.
Love lives in a human heart.

Annabell Naeb (9)
Clifton Without Junior School

EXTINCT BUT STILL LIVING IN MY MIND

An extinct sleeper,
A secret keeper.

A loud howler,
A high-pitched growler.

A tail swisher,
A freedom wisher.

A meat eater,
A pleasant greeter.

A long yawner,
A distant caller.

A quick pacer,
A rabbit chaser.

A creature you will never find
A distant memory in my mind.

Tasmanian wolf.

Megan Williams (10)
Clifton Without Junior School

McDONALD'S

A Happy Meal maker,
A teenage employer,
A burger lover,
A chip breeder,
A people feeder,
A fast food leader.

Liam Spencer (11)
Clifton Without Junior School

DUSK, NIGHT AND SUNRISE

Dusk falls
Orange, pink skies
Birds return to their nests
Night is drawing nearer, nearer,
Earth sleeps . . .

Night falls
Cold, bitter air
Golden twinkling stars
Owls hoot far in the distant fields
Full moon . . .

Sunrise
Golden, hot sphere
A blank world lights up as
Sunbeams pour over the horizon
Awake . . .

Rachael Smithson (11)
Clifton Without Junior School

ALARM CLOCK

A morning lover,
A happiness snatcher.

A sleep waker,
A dream taker.

A misery maker,
A person traitor.

Rebecca Clark (10)
Clifton Without Junior School

MIRROR

There once was a very gleaming mirror,
Hidden away in a corner of an attic.

One day a poor man looked through the mirror
And saw a home for life.

A hippie peered through the mirror
And saw world peace.

A believer looked through the mirror
And saw aliens land on Earth.

A little child peered through the mirror
And saw a pet dog.

A captain looked through the mirror
And saw dry land.

A soldier peeped through the mirror
And saw war end.

Then a millionaire looked through the mirror,
And the mirror cracked.

James Secker (11)
Clifton Without Junior School

LOVE

Love is pink,
It smells like rose flowers.
Love tastes like clean air,
It sounds slow and peaceful,
It feels smooth.
Love lives in a flower garden.

Lydia Wharton (9)
Clifton Without Junior School

THE ROOM OF NIGHTMARES

There once was a room of nightmares
Made from everybody's bad dreams.

One dark, windy night an otter looked into the room
And saw extinction.

A soldier gazed into the room
And saw pictures of World War III.

A nurse stared into the room
And saw the plague.

An old lady looked into the room
And saw loneliness.

An ocean peered into the room
And saw an oil slick.

Becky Postlethwaite (11)
Clifton Without Junior School

I LOVE GUINEA PIGS

Guinea pigs squeal.
Guinea pigs eat their meals.
Guinea pigs are sweet.
Guinea pigs are nice to meet.
Guinea pigs in the run.
Guinea pigs having fun.
Up and down they go
Sometimes fast, sometimes slow.

Sophie Linley (10)
Clifton Without Junior School

A Dog

A deafening barker,
A petrifying howler,
An energetic chaser,
A powerful wagger,
A sloppy licker,
A champion biter,
A springy bouncer,
A play dead trickster,
A toy retriever,
An affectionate communicator.

A dogalogue to make me a dog!

Suzanne Goodwin (11)
Clifton Without Junior School

Guess What

A wet licker,
A lazy sleeper.

A playful growler,
A tickle lover.

A tail wiggler,
A fast runner.

A disgusting eater,
A super survivor.

Eloise McCombe (10)
Clifton Without Junior School

A TV SCREEN

There was a TV screen hidden in a corner.

One day the paper boy stared through a TV
And all the dogs were friendly.

A teacher gazed into a TV
And saw a class so not even a noise of a child was heard.

God inspected the TV
And saw peace everywhere.

Refugees searched through a TV
And saw a home for themselves.

Aaron Williams (11)
Clifton Without Junior School

MIRROR

There once was a gleaming mirror tucked away
In the corner of a dusty attic.

One afternoon a soldier looked through the mirror
And saw there were no wars.

A vet gazed through the mirror
And saw all the animals playing joyfully.

A dentist stared into the mirror
And spotted lots of clean teeth.

Stacey Thackeray-Sleight (11)
Clifton Without Junior School

THE MIRROR

There was once a very small mirror,
Hidden away in a corner of a stable.

One day a farmer looked through the mirror
And saw a bright blue X-reg tractor.

A teacher stared through the mirror
And saw her student being a teacher in the future.

A rocket scientist gaped through the mirror
And saw a massive rocket created by himself.

A lonely man peeked through the mirror
And saw a wife.

A fish peered through the mirror
And saw a huge amount of pellets.

A vet gawped through the mirror
And saw happy animals.

A mouse peeked through the mirror
And saw a huge pile of cheese.

Tom Smallwood (10)
Clifton Without Junior School

PAIN

Pain is a deep purple,
It smells like a rotten plum.
Pain tastes like tears of unhappiness
It sounds like a volcano erupting,
It feels like scratching and tearing.
Pain lives in the hand of a giant.

Claire Heslop (8)
Clifton Without Junior School

SUMMER AND AUTUMN

Summer!
Glistening sun
Splashing in cool oceans
Making playful footprints in the sand
Clear skies.

Autumn!
Dry leaves falling
Dancing flames leap all around us
Chilly nights assault us again.

Lucy Coates (11)
Clifton Without Junior School

BALLET DREAMS

As I dance towards the bright light,
It brings back memories of the sun setting,
Seasons turning and time ticking on slowly
At its own pace, during lessons in the dance hall.

But now I'm on stage I only want to dance,
The blurred faces of the audience wave and chant,
They chant my name
'Rosie, Rosie, Rosie, what are you doing?'

I look around me,
I'm back in the dance hall
But I'm sitting down, I was dreaming.
I'm still in Grade One, I've got a little way to go yet.

Rosie O'Grady (10)
Fishergate CP School

MAGIC SPELL

Work the magic,
It would be tragic,
If this magic spell didn't work.

Magic, magic, make it magic,
Work the magic and make it work.
Stir the potion,
It would be a commotion,
If this potion didn't work.

Make it work,
The potion and the spell.
Please, please, please,
Make it work well.

Magic, magic make it magic,
Work the magic and make it work.
Stir the potion,
It would be a commotion,
If this potion didn't work.

Francesca Day (10)
Fishergate CP School

REMAINS

As we swim through a lagoon of placid darkness
We are slowly devoured into our own hellhole.
We are swallowed by internal monsters
Eating away at our already darkened souls.
Lightness lives as a shining star, slowly withering away.
It is our fault.
There is no better place but this world could be so . . .

Joe Finch (10)
Fishergate CP School

THE SEASONS

Summer

Summer is a time for fun,
A time to be happy and warm.
The beach with cool blue sea and yellow crystal sand.

Spring

Spring is a time to see new life and smells in the air.
The smell of freshly cut grass and tulips
And the noise of children laughing and shouting.

Autumn

Autumn is a time to crunch in the leaves and play with conkers.
A time to be happy and excited and
A time to dress up like ghouls for Hallowe'en.

Winter

Winter is a time to wrap up warm in your hat and gloves.
A time to look forward to Christmas
Opening all your presents.

Erin McKelvey-Williams (10)
Fishergate CP School

THE BEACH AND THE OCEAN

Splashy, blue ocean water calmly rises to my feet
Waves can be big and waves can be small,
Listen to the splashes, look at the shells,
Rocks in the ocean which come to the beach,
Sealife swims through the ocean,
There is sand at the bottom of the ocean and sand on the beach.

Anya Price (8)
Fishergate CP School

THE TOOTHLESS TIGER

The toothless tiger sits in a cage,
He always seems to look very aged,
Eating stale bread only once a day,
He never seems to think to play,
I don't know why he's such a spoilsport,
I wish he was more alive and young,
Maybe he would someday talk,
A hero perhaps, but only unsung,
Then suddenly! One marvellous day,
A miracle! Oh no! Hah hay!
He grows his teeth to forever stay,
I feel happy with him, and I shout, 'Hurray!'

Emily Denison (9)
Fishergate CP School

SEASONS

Icicles hang sharp and sheer,
Snow falls softly to the ground.
Flowers bloom like you and I,
Birds start singing their lovely sound
The sun sizzles down to Earth
It's summer holidays for us again
Leaves crunch under our feet,
This time of year there's lots of rain!

Lily Charnock (8)
Fishergate CP School

IN A DREAM

Off I go, I'm floating away up to the soft, warm clouds
Where I sleep until day.
I have good dreams all night long,
Dreaming I'm dancing to my favourite song.

In a dream the best things happen . . .
You could become a pop star and you could do ya rappin'!

But then the horra' suddenly strikes
I wake up and it's
    Tomorra!

Rachel Musgrave (11)
Fishergate CP School

THE ARCTIC

Bleak, desolate wasteland
White Sahara of the north
Icebergs float in pools of sorrow
Swans on an icy lake.
Shipwrecks lie in the frozen deep
Silent tombs of death
Slumbering like fireside cats for all time.
Snowflakes swoop aimlessly
Jagged beauty in each one
Savage polar bears rule the ice
Frozen splendour at the edge of the Earth.

Lydia Onyett (9)
Fishergate CP School

SEASONS

Spring, summer, autumn, winter,
All these are different seasons.

Spring is when the plants grow,
And the sky can make a rainbow.

Summer is when the sun comes out,
And everyone can run about.

Autumn is when the leaves fall,
And the wind begins to call.

Winter is when the snow comes,
And we go to see our mums.

Spring, summer, autumn, winter,
All these are different seasons.

Alex Perry (8)
Fishergate CP School

THE PERFECT WORLD

Kind and helpful,
Caring, good,
Nobody daring, behaving the way they should,
Good people speaking nice things,
Loving and hugging, dancing with friends
Nobody shouting or fighting these are in a
Perfect world.

Hannah Skeet (9)
Fishergate CP School

BAD KIDS

Children at school
Break every rule,
They call each other names
And play disruptive games,
They yell at all the teachers
The ugliest of creatures,
Then worst of all
They throw paintballs at the wall!

Jessie Morris (9)
Fishergate CP School

BABY ELEPHANT

The baby elephant
A smaller version of his mother
Elephant, elephant small but strong,
Stepping in his mother's footprints
Trying not to trip over his trunk,
But don't go near his mother
A slight whip from her trunk
Could bring a long and dreadful death.

The baby elephant
Splashing in the silent waters
Then he is free no more
Taken into captivity
Surrounded by people
Being forced to pull logs
Shut in a cage away from his mother
His tusks cut to a stump
He is longing to be free.

Rachel Huke Danter (10)
Forest Of Galtres Primary School

THE CHEETAH

The world is at his mercy,
Sprinting, attacking, killing
It takes after his prey
At the speed of lightning
He catches his victim
All is now still.

Drought is a better killer,
So thinks the cheetah
Thin as a pipe cleaner,
As it craves for food.

The world dims in his eyes,
As the cheetah draws his last breath.

Thomas Wood (10)
Forest Of Galtres Primary School

EAGLE

Graceful eagle,
Skimming the surface of the peaceful lake,
The king of birds.

Swooping silently at his frightened prey,
Ruffling his feathers importantly,
Stretching his magnificent wings.

Silhouetted against the moon,
Swooping, twirling, twisting,
Then resting.
Waiting for morning to dawn again.

Lucy Rooke (10)
Forest Of Galtres Primary School

RHINO

Rhino, rhino every creature's nightmare,
Rhino, rhino, the ability to crush
The ability to destroy
The ability to bring death
Whenever he charges he will never give up
There will be no mercy.

Rhino, rhino a thorn in every creature's heart,
Rhino, rhino the ability to smash,
The ability to destroy,
The ability to bring death
The slightest movement will send him into a rage,
There will be no mercy.

Ben Stirk (10)
Forest Of Galtres Primary School

THE WIND IS . . .

The wind is like fire,
Calm and quiet,
Building up, getting stronger,
Crackling, killing and destroying,
Until the rain comes,
Fire and rain at war,
As the rain settles the fire comes back again,
Disrupting everything in sight,
Eventually it flutters silently down the road.

Rosie Heartshorne (10)
Forest Of Galtres Primary School

SHARK

Dangerous swimmer
His eyes searching the seas
While he glides through the deep waters.

Frightened small fish
Wary of the king of the ocean
Hide among the rocks.

Unseeing creatures
Not knowing the danger
Swim openly in the sea.

Sudden murderer
Catching his victim
Back to his secretive lair.

David Runciman (9)
Forest Of Galtres Primary School

THE WIND IS A . . .

The wind is a heartbreaker
At times it can be calm
When it is furious,
A tornado appears in the sky
It rips, it tears, it sucks people up.

When the destruction is over,
It quietens down,
Not a whisper is heard out of him again.

Jessica Johnson (10)
Forest Of Galtres Primary School

THE WIND

Howling wind
Appearing from nowhere
Destroying everything in its path,
Cars trying to stay put
Taking roofs off people's houses
Howling wind,
Humans insulated inside their own homes.
Howling wind,
Terrifying elderly people,
Creating terrible storms at sea,
Sinking ships,
Creating havoc in the city
Then . . . the next day all is quiet,
The world is at peace once again.

Christopher Duckwith (10)
Forest Of Galtres Primary School

THE WIND

The wind is a silent ghost
As it manoeuvres through the trees
And riots through people's hair
Then it turns into a tornado and sniffs
Out the dustbin
And in despair nudges it over
Along with all the rubbish
And silently slithers away.

Alistair Rathmell (10)
Forest Of Galtres Primary School

THE DOLPHIN

Gently the dolphin
Jumping, leaping, splashing
Catches everyone's eye
Children glare through the glass,
At the bottom of the boat,
How fascinated they look,
Gently the dolphin
Calling to family and friends.

Rebecca Clark (10)
Forest Of Galtres Primary School

THE PENGUIN

The penguin in its igloo shivers
Penguin, penguin
Swooping into the sea
Catching, catching the fish
Dying of old age, passing cruelty
Penguin is now gone.

Amy McGuinness
Forest Of Galtres Primary School

THE WIND . . .

The wind is an angry Hoover,
Snatching the litter,
Swishing, swishing
But when it is time
The wind rapidly moves on.

Lydia Huggins (10)
Forest Of Galtres Primary School

SLOWLY THE SNOW

Slowly the snow
Creeping out
Of the midnight sky
Covering everything
In its path
Emerging from nowhere.

Shaun Belt (9)
Forest Of Galtres Primary School

THE PIG

Gentle hunger,
His small tail plays on the mud
Pig waits for his meat to shred
Bit by bit the pig jumps with excitement
The pig is wild, charging at the barrier
He settles down to sleep.

Chris Palmer (9)
Forest Of Galtres Primary School

BAT

Bat, bat flying
Bat, bat, swooping, swooping
Ducking, darting, twirling and twisting
He is searching for his food, it's way past dinner time
Where he flies little mice run to hide!

Libby Ashton (9)
Forest Of Galtres Primary School

WILD PONIES

Galloping in the air
Hundreds of them in the New Forest park,
Nothing else is there except them.

Babies born,
Hundreds of them in the New Forest park,
Bounding with their mothers.

Look around,
Hundreds of them in the New Forest park
They're everywhere to be seen.

Sarah Louise Ruddock (10)
Forest Of Galtres Primary School

THE BOAR

Roughly the boar jaggedly
Drags itself through
The clammy and waxy jungle
Panting with blood on its tusks,
As it slows down
It hears a scamper across the ground
It takes his interest,
It moves slower than ever
It hears a crunch and looks
But all is quiet and still.

Thomas Stones (10)
Forest Of Galtres Primary School

THE WIND IS A SPEEDING CHEETAH

The wind is a speeding cheetah,
Speeding everywhere, seeking his prey
He pounces out of a bush,
To catch his dinner
Devouring so fast and silently
Yet he's still hungry
He waits in the dark for his next victim.

Jake Campbell
Forest Of Galtres Primary School

THE FISH

The fish
Glides through the water
Searching, looking, hearing
Lonely and lost
He finally finds his way
To his long-lost friends.

Harriet Long (10)
Forest Of Galtres Primary School

THE ELEPHANT

Elephant as strong as a tree
He stamps like a herd of boars
He will kill a human with his trunk
He will knock down a tree
With his bare trunk.

Steven Frost (10)
Forest Of Galtres Primary School

I'M ON THE MOON

I didn't expect this . . .
Silence surrounds me
I'm trapped with *no* sound,
The ground is as grey as an elephant
The rocks are as sharp as a knife
The sharp cold hits me like a thousand spikes.
I can see Earth like an emerald and ocean blue crystal.
I look into a dead sky with a glinting gold shooting star,
No houses
It's barren
Nothing lives on the moon
The floor is just like grey sand
The Earth beckons me back
My heart belongs there.

Josh Turner (9)
Hob Moor Junior School

THE SILENT WORLD

The moon is dust, cold like my grandma's hair.

It feels like I am all alone on a freezing world.

Listen, listen to the silence of the deep black space.

The Earth looks like an emerald and ocean blue marble.

From here I can see Pluto where it should be.

Earth's beckoning me home.

Tempting me to leave this silent world.

David Jefferson (9)
Hob Moor Junior School

THE BATTLE OF STRENGTH

The night closes on us
As the whale's blue kingdom takes us to our next challenge
The night lets go
And releases the sunbeams,
Dawn has finally come.
I suddenly see
Where my challenge must be
Ahead of me
The land where my battle must begin.
As I finally reach the God's world
I see my battle is not going to be as I thought.
With my warriors I am sure not to lose.
We have crushed our enemies
The ravens come and take their spirits to Valhalla
It is silent as the waves travel me home.

Jamie Akers (8)
Hob Moor Junior School

THE DUSTY MOON

Not a whisper, not a wind or gentle breeze
This is the moon
All dry and dusty
So lonely this is
All dark and eerie like a skeleton
Craters as large as Big Foot's feet,
Pointing rocks like sharp daggers,
Something is going to happen
The Earth beckons me home.

Ellise Melia (9)
Hob Moor Junior School

A Quietness On The Moon

The moon is dusty and silent
It feels really weird
Listen it is really silent
I'm not scared.
But all alone
I move like a tortoise
From here I can see the Earth really small.
The Earth looks like a crystal
I'm not scared of anything
There is less gravity here
The craters are a lot like small volcanoes ready to burst
The Earth beckons me back home
There is no atmosphere on the moon.

Brian Kent (8)
Hob Moor Junior School

The Silent Moon

The moon is dusty and cold
Hanging in the darkness of space
Silence covers the barren land.

I feel frozen, as fear runs up my spine
I'm so amazed by this empty place
There's no air to live or breathe
I look to see the rockets pass by
Leaving a golden glinting trail.

Earth beckons me home
Slowly, as the night disappears
Like the cruiser into black space.

Jade James (9)
Hob Moor Junior School

ON THE MOON

The moon is all dusty and dry
Just like sand all grey
It's cold and getting colder
Not warm
Not even any air
Listen, it is so silent you can even hear a pin drop
I can see the other planets I shout 'Hello'
But nothing is said out of my breath
The Earth looks like a glass glowing ball
All shining green and blue
I must go and say goodbye
I go off jumping to my rocket.

Ellie Passmore (8)
Hob Moor Junior School

THE ARID MOON

It's dry, dusty and arid,
I feel slow,
I hardly move,
And see nothing but glistening stars.

I see Earth
A beautiful, shining emerald
Craters,
Some look like footprints.

I see mountains
Tall,
Wide,
I do nothing but stare as Earth beckons me home.

Martin Scadding (9)
Hob Moor Junior School

THE ORANG-UTAN

The orang-utan swings from tree to tree,
He lives in the rainforest
Free so free,
So cute and cuddly to me
Yes me,
He's rustling in a bush or a tree.

They're fighting over food to eat,
They clean each other sweet
So sweet,
Scavenging high and low
But don't cheat, don't cheat,
There, over there, a noise I hear,
I know what it is, it's an
Orang-utan!

Victoria Johnson (11)
Husthwaite CE Primary School

AUTUMN

Red robins chirping
Misty fog floating
Bare trees swaying
Warm sun shining
Grey squirrels searching
Freezing frost cracking
Soaking rain spitting
Blue sky clearing
Cold wind howling
Icy snow slipping.

Amy Marsh (9)
Husthwaite CE Primary School

ELEPHANT

The elephant moves his stumpy feet
His wrinkled body slumbers by,
His secret smile, hidden by his trunk
He glances over with his small eye
His wretched body comes to a halt,
His rough lace for tail goes swish, swash
But inside he is an unknown warrior.

He moves once more with a great heave
Smiling with a tiny frown,
With his feet he slowly pounds
The ground booms
He starts to run,
Looking for a refreshment
To heal his wounds
For inside he is an unknown warrior.

Rebecca Scarce (11)
Husthwaite CE Primary School

AUTUMN

Flaming bonfire burns
Cold wind howling
Dazzling fireworks sparkling
Wet rain leaking
Brown leaves falling
Warm sun burning
Crunchy chestnuts growing
Chilly frost freezing
Scary Hallowe'en spooking.

Bethany Atkinson (9)
Husthwaite CE Primary School

A WEEK OF WINTER WEATHER

On Monday crisp, sparkling, patterned frost.
On Tuesday misty, cloudy, thick fog.
On Wednesday crisp, cold, white snow.
On Thursday wet, drizzly, spitting rain.
On Friday sludgy, grey, mucky sleet.
On Saturday cold, glittery, shiny ice.
On Sunday dreary, foggy, murky, mist.

A week
A week
Of winter
Weather.

Charles Ramsay, Paul Scott,
Nina Bernard & Frances Craddock
Husthwaite CE Primary School

ICE SKATING

I was loads better than her,
He wobbles around the arena.
I skated gracefully over the ice,
He tripped over his feet and fell on his bum.
Everyone clapped at my amazing skills,
Everyone laughed at his clumsiness.
Everyone thought she was rubbish,
He had to sit out half the time, because of his injuries.
As I left the manager asked me to sign up for lessons,
As he left the manager told him never to come again.

Sarah Jackson (11)
Husthwaite CE Primary School

A WEEK OF WINTER WEATHER

On Monday crisp, sparkling, patterned frost.
On Tuesday white, crispy, flaky snow.
On Wednesday dripping, drizzling, damp rain.
On Thursday foggy, cloudy frost.
On Friday sunny, rain, cloudy rainbow.
On Saturday snow, windy, hailstones and slush.
On Sunday slippery, slidey, dangerous ice.

A week
A week
Of winter weather.

Simon Taylor (8)
Husthwaite CE Primary School

AUTUMN

Crinkly leaves fluttering,
Dead plants drooping,
Bare trees dying, sadly.

Rainy weather raining,
Hot sun burning,
Blowy wind blowing, roughly.

Food harvest cutting corn,
Ghosts spooky Hallowe'en trick or treating
Guy Fawkes, Bonfire Night celebrating.

Hollie Suff (10)
Husthwaite CE Primary School

A WEEK OF WINTER WEATHER

On Monday crisp, sparkling pattern.
On Tuesday sparkly, cold, white snow.
On Wednesday grey, windy, freezing rain.
On Thursday brown, icy, slushy snow.
On Friday wet, rainy, saturated ground.
On Saturday spotting, spitting, drizzling rain.
On Sunday damp, crispy hailstone.

A week
A week
Of winter weather.

Adéle Attrill (8)
Husthwaite CE Primary School

AUTUMN POEM

Golden leaves crumbling
Bare trees swaying
Brown chestnuts falling
Fluffy squirrels racing
Sapphire foxes hunting
Grey rabbits scurrying
Brown acorns splitting
Crazy Hallowe'en creeping
Flaming bonfire sparkling
Dead plants dropping.

Naomi Davies (10)
Husthwaite CE Primary School

THE BUTTERFLY

The butterfly fluttered, flapping her
golden wings, with colourful bright
blues and pinks. With fumes of
flowers as she takes off and
flutters higher and higher
until she's out of reach,
but then she gracefully flitters
down and lands.

She clicks her legs together,
and a gentle sound of slish, slash
as she sucks. Her scent comes again,
this time stronger, she glints and glitters
in the sunshine, until the last glint
comes, and she flutters out of sight.

Amelia de Wend Fenton (10)
Husthwaite CE Primary School

NATURE NUMBERS

One old orange obedient octopus.
Two trendy tiptoeing tortoises.
Three trampolining tigers.
Four fantastically funny frogs.
Five flipping forgetful flamingos.
Six silly sausage seals.
Seven sour stupid silent salmon.
Eight enormous envelope-eating elephants.
Nine naughty nibbling newts.
Ten table tennis tapping tadpoles.

Nikita Norman (8)
Husthwaite CE Primary School

LION

A lonesome lion prowls the plain
Peering and looking for a pride
Smelling of decaying skin and ponging of prey
He lies and listens, watches and waits
He jumps joyfully at what he sees,
A bunch of buffalo, to his glee.

In one swift motion he moves forward
Only a couple of feet at first
He races up into a run
The buffalo scatter back and forward, back and sideways
He sinks his teeth through its skin
Dinner is served, it is very much dead.

William Metcalfe (11)
Husthwaite CE Primary School

THE AUTUMN POEM

Flaming bonfire burns.
Brown leaves falling.
Dazzling fireworks sparkling.
And all the birds calling.

Warm sun burning.
Wet rain leaking.
Chilly frost freezing.
And all the creatures peeking.

Brian Stebbings (10)
Husthwaite CE Primary School

FIREWORKS

Fiery swirls in the sky
Indigo, orange, blue, green and red
Rising high and then they bang
Catherine wheels swirl round and round
Overhead rockets zoom, bang!
Rusted fencing burn Guy Fawkes to a cinder
Excited children hold their bright sparklers.
The dark sky is lit with glimmering
Stars and the moon.
Cries and laughter all around
Torches streak the sky
Gunpowder fills the air with a smoky odour
The smell of hot food makes us all hungry
Crackling fire smoulders.

Natalie Brown (11)
Husthwaite CE Primary School

AUTUMN

Crunchy leaves falling
Cold wind spinning
Heavy rain pouring
Misty fog disappearing
Prickly hedgehogs hibernating
White clouds fluffy
Swaying trees moving
Spiky frost dripping.

Sarah Fleming (9)
Husthwaite CE Primary School

AUTUMN

Old trees creaking
Orange leaves rustling
Red fox killing
Black wolf howling.

Hot bonfire crackling
Colourful fireworks banging
Black badger burrowing
Spiky hedgehog hibernating

Black Hallowe'en haunting
Round pumpkin glowing
Spotty deer standing
Friendly squirrel leaping

White mist clearing
Slippery ice melting
Fluffy clouds floating
Burning sun boiling.

Abbie Burnett (9)
Husthwaite CE Primary School

HARVEST

H ibernation of animals
A pples falling off trees
R ipe fruit
V egetables
E normous
S trawberries are ready to eat
T hank you for harvest.

Kirsty Wood (11)
Husthwaite CE Primary School

NANNY

All I have got left is memories,
But I really want her.
My nanny meant so much to me,
If only she was here now.
She had no hatred inside her,
Only a soft, kind heart,
I feel that I have lost so much.

I feel that I have lost one of the most important
People that I had.
She had so many friends.
And all of them loved her so much.
If only she would come back and
Stay for a bit longer.

She cared so much for everyone,
And I bet she still does.
Most people knew her and knew
That she was too kind.
I cried for her for weeks,
If only she would come back.
I feel like a big part of me is lonely.

Ria Bernard (10)
Husthwaite CE Primary School

AUTUMN

Crunchy leaves blowing, warm
Sizzling bonfire. Furry animals
Hibernating. Frosty plants dying.
Bare trees bending, dark spooky
Hallowe'en, bright fireworks whizzing.

Alex Norman (10)
Husthwaite CE Primary School

AUTUMN

Old trees creaking
Hot fire creeping
Friendly squirrel leaping
Muddy floods flowing
Round pumpkin glowing

Grey wolf howling
White mist clearing
Wet rain flooding
Hot sun burning
Fluffy clouds floating

Slippery ice freezing
Spotty deer staring
Red fox hunting.

Christopher Price (9)
Husthwaite CE Primary School

AUTUMN POEM

Grey rabbits racing
Brown leaves dropping
Bear trees swaying
Brown acorns splitting
Spooky Hallowe'en creeping
Yellow bonfire flaming
Furry squirrels finding
Sapphire foxes hunting
Brown chestnuts falling
Orange fireworks flying.

Samantha Brack (9)
Husthwaite CE Primary School

MY DOG

I have a dog
And her name is Tess
I walk her
Pat her
Play with her
Feed her.

I care for her
Love her
Cuddle her
I have a dog
And her fur is chocolate.

Sophie Lawrance (10)
Husthwaite CE Primary School

AUTUMN

Blowing wind howling,
Wet rain drips,
Cotton woolly clouds float.

Yellow leaves fall,
Brown acorns falling,
Sparkling bonfires burning,

Hibernating hedgehogs sleep,
Red squirrels squeaking,
Grey rabbits hopping.

Louisa Hood (10)
Husthwaite CE Primary School

AUTUMN

Colourful fireworks crashing
Hot bonfire crackling
White clouds floating
Orange leaves setting

Brown pumpkin flickering
White mist clearing
Slippery ice melting
Fluffy cloud floating.

Old trees creaking
Wet rain pouring
Spotty deer standing
Friendly squirrel leaping.

Spiky hedgehog hibernating
Black badger tunnelling
Red fox pouncing
Grey horse cantering.

Celia Craddock (10)
Husthwaite CE Primary School

AUTUMN

Blowing winds howling
Grey rabbits hopping
Red squirrels squeaking
Sparkling bonfire burning
Fluffy clouds moving
Wet rain dripping
Deep floods rising
Green acorns falling.

Joe Walker (10)
Husthwaite CE Primary School

MY PET DOG TRIX

It's not the same without her,
No dribbling on the chairs,
No licking the roast dinner
And no barking in the night.

It's not the same without her,
She's not there to sleep on the end of my bed
Or chew my school clothes
Or lick my face.

It's not the same without her,
I can't go for walkies with her,
Just sit at home with a bag of crisps not sharing them.

It's not the same without her,
No lead, no collar, no bones
And no following me to school,
I miss Trix very much.

Lisa-Marie Munford (10)
Husthwaite CE Primary School

AUTUMN

Crackling leaves falling
Cold wind blowing
Prickly hedgehogs hibernating
Sparkly frost dripping
Heavy rain pounding
Swaying trees moving
Fluffy white clouds
Misty fog dripping.

Charlotte Kingsley (9)
Husthwaite CE Primary School

AUTUMN POEM

Dreaded trees swaying
White foxes howling
Quick squirrels scuttering
Sparkling bonfire flaming
Spooky Hallowe'en scaring
Grey rabbits racing
Boiled chestnuts chattering
Brown leaves crumbling
Brown acorns falling
Orange leaves dropping
Dead trees falling
Gold sparks flying
Blue sky closes up.

Callum Watt (9)
Husthwaite CE Primary School

AUTUMN

Blowing wind howling
Brown leaves falling
Sleeping hedgehogs hibernating
Grey rabbits hopping
Chilling snow falling
Hot sun warming
Feathery pheasants flying
Cotton wool clouds floating
Red squirrels chatting
Wet dripping rain.

Katie Clarke (9)
Husthwaite CE Primary School

AUTUMN

Wet rain puddling
Muddy flood flowing
White mist clearing
Cold frost freezing.

Fluffy cloud floating
Slippery ice melting
Old trees creaking
Orange leaves settling.

Scary Hallowe'en haunting
Round pumpkin glowing
Hot bonfire crackling
Colourful fireworks banging.

Warm sun sizzling
Spotty deer standing
Friendly squirrels leaping
Spiky hedgehogs hibernating.

Black badger tunnelling
Red fox killing
Grey wolf howling.

Harry Wise (10)
Husthwaite CE Primary School

AUTUMN

Crunchy leaves blowing
Warm sizzling bonfire
Furry animals hibernating
Frosty plants, bare trees
Bending.

James Lawrance (9)
Husthwaite CE Primary School

AUTUMN

Crackling leaves falling,
Sparkling frost dripping,
Misty fog disappearing,
Heavy rain pouring,
Cold wind spinning,
Swaying trees bending,
Shivering squirrels hibernating,
Cold hedgehogs sleeping,
Grey rabbits bouncing.

Bridie Doy (9)
Husthwaite CE Primary School

MY SECRET VOYAGE

I think on my secret voyage
I'll go by ship.
I'll have a dip
In the tranquil sea.

I think on my secret voyage
I'll go by car.
I'll get very far
And sing to the radio.

I think on my secret voyage
I'll go by bus.
But we'll have to rush
To get to my secret voyage.

Aimee Pearcy (11)
Osbaldwick Primary School

My Feet

I wish my feet were beautiful
as beautiful as beautiful
(but you never know
when they might come in useful)

I wish my feet were beautiful
As beautiful as can be
Just like everybody else's
But not like me.

I wish my feet were beautiful
As beautiful as yours
I think I will give up now
And just look at yours.

Jason Hollis (11)
Osbaldwick Primary School

Thunder And Lightning

Oh look, and there goes
Thunder again.
And now, here comes the
Lightning.
Wow, that was a big
Flash.
Hahh, the thunder's getting
Really loud now.

They've been fighting for an hour,
Ha, thunder keep it down.
And lightning stop flashing
My eyes are really hurting.

Chloe Jones (10)
Osbaldwick Primary School

MY VOYAGE

I wanted to go on a voyage to Mars,
To create my own spaceship and fly with the stars.
I found an old box with a cone on the top,
I had my own rocket before I could stop.

The travel was brilliant that's all I can say,
I wish I could go there just every day!
But what could I do when my spaceship broke down?
I crashed down to Earth with a mighty big frown.

My rocket was broken, crashed out on the floor,
My mum heard the bang and she started to roar.
She told me off for the terrible mess,
And shouted because I had ruined my dress.

I promised my mum that the travelling would stop,
That I'd do girlie things like helping to shop.
I'll stop down here with the buses and cars,
And never again will I go to Mars.
(But I might try Venus.)

Rachael Umpleby (11)
Osbaldwick Primary School

DON'T ROCK ON YOUR CHAIR

'Don't rock on your chair'
The teacher said
'Or you'll fall back
and damage your head.'

'Don't rock on your chair'
the head teacher did beg
'Or you'll fall back and
break your leg.'

'Don't rock on your chair'
my mother hissed
'Or you'll fall back
and break your wrist.'

'Don't rock back on your chair'
my father said
'Or you'll fall back
and then you'll be dead!'

Sophie Winship (10)
Osbaldwick Primary School

THE VOYAGE

The ship is tossing like a coin,
Through the high tides it crashes;
A bumper car at a fairground.
On a voyage to a far-off land,
Find some gold glistening like the depths of the sea.
Seaweed like the arms of a savage;
Reaching high, curling and swirling as slippery as soap.
The shore has gone, in the distance, never to return.
A werewolf is howling,
A full moon is shining as white as a baby's tooth.
The tide is rising,
The waves banging on the ship's door.
The voyage is over,
A shipwreck washed up on the shore.
A failure.
All is lost.

Claire Morley (10)
Osbaldwick Primary School

MY SECRET VOYAGE

Last night I imagined fantasies far away,
In unique dark districts;
Each one with its own specific secret.

First I was hiking,
Through an impenetrable and murky jungle;
Lashing my way through firm vines,
I tried to scream but they evolved around me;
Like a long-armed creature, hard as concrete.

Suddenly, I was rowing,
In a wooden, dilapidated boat,
Across the opaque waters of rippling and writhing snakes,
As they hissed and splashed like bombs in a minefield.

Next I was sprinting through orchard bare,
Stumbling and tumbling as branches from trees loomed over me;
They were dark, eerie shadows everlasting; like God.

Last of all I was flying through the sky,
On a magical unicorn to a scary unnamed planet;
Unconfined and lifeless, the sky extending down on me;
But never trapping me, like a blind swamp monster,
Stretching its deformed hands in the shady sunlight.

Finally, I landed, my wings dissolving,
Like a warm salt solution,
Ready for another tranquil dream;
    Another night . . .
I had reached my true destination.

Rebecca Ward (10)
Osbaldwick Primary School

ORCAS

Orcas are my favourite animals.
When they leap, jump and breach,
They look as if they are dancing.
Orcas are the predators of the sea,
They only weigh five tonnes.
Their black and white colours
Prove a camouflage,
Through the dark mists.

Nicola Bradshaw (9)
St George's RC School

LITTLE TIM

The worst offence of Little Tim
Was sitting on the biscuit tin.
But all at once the tin shattered
And Little Tim got bruised and battered
His mum and dad fainted at the sight
Of Little Tim's biscuit flight.

Thomas Khan (8)
St George's RC School

MY FAMOUS GRAN

My famous gran always went for a run,
Eating a big fat bun.
When she stopped,
She always hopped,
Then she said 'What great fun.'

Ieuan Solanki (9)
St George's RC School

MY DAD

My dad he is tall and round,
My dad has bold blue eyes,
He scampers around the house,
It seems to my friends that
He's really strange,
But I love him with all my
Big, cuddly, squishy heart.

Stephanie Ireland (9)
St George's RC School

MY DOLLY

I have a dolly,
Her name is Polly,
In the rain,
She has a brolly,
In the sun,
She has a lolly,
All day,
She is very jolly.

Charlotte Holmes (9)
St George's RC School

HOLIDAY

Sun beam,
Across the stream.
Wind so still,
The weather's brill.
Grass so delicate and clean.

Megan Simpson (9)
St George's RC School

GEORGE CLOONEY

There was a problem with George Clooney.
He danced about as if he was a loony.
He danced around the town all night
Giving all the people a nasty fright.
One day he fell into the river
The people stopped and saw him shiver.
Then he did something he shouldn't have done,
Then an eel came and bit his bum.

Chantelle Burn (9)
St George's RC School

MY WEEK

I moan on Monday,
I time on Tuesday,
I wail on Wednesday,
I think on Thursday,
I fly on Friday,
I sing on Saturday,
And I sail on Sunday.

Lauren Lea Husband (9)
St George's RC School

SUNSET HAIKU

Boat running quickly
Sun setting behind the sea
Fish swimming slowly.

Charlotte Ellis (9)
St George's RC School

THE MOOR

The wind was a roaring torrent
but all she heard was silence,
silence over the moor.

The rain grew ever bitter,
but all she felt was silence,
silence over the moor.

The lightning flashed brighter,
but all she saw was silence,
silence over the moor.

Rachael Anderson (9)
St George's RC School

MY GRANDMA'S DOG

My grandma's dog barks and bites,
So she'd rather go to Mars.
When her bally gets taken away,
She knocks you down and thinks,
She's found the perfect play thingy
She licks and then she spits.
When she makes her ball hit the radiator
And shouts 'ro, ro, rot ball'
I'm sure she means, 'It's a goal!'

Maddy Burrows (8)
St George's RC School

SEVEN AGES OF MAN

As an infant I'm dependant upon my parents
to guide, clothe, protect and care for me.

School days have arrived greeted with mixed emotion
but survive I will and meet with challenges one by one.

I then discover that girls are important
particularly one to share my dreams with.

Full of passion, honour and brave deeds hoping for
victory to come soon, comfortably off, mature? And ready to play a part
in someone's life.

Tired and weary I am ready to give responsibility
over to a younger man, no longer useful I give in.

Jonathan Bairstow (11)
St Olave's School

EXAMINATION

Walk into the room
Scary like a doom
Pick up the pen,
And wished he was in his den.

Brain ticking
Clock flicking
Imagination around the room
Zooming like a witch's broom

Panicking stare, the teachers loom
Questions revealing nothing but gloom.

Sylvia Lai Mun Wong (10)
St Olave's School

FRUIT

That's a big juicy melon on the table,
It looks so nice to eat,
With its juicy insides and smooth outsides
It's gotta be nice to eat.
Oh yes, that's a big, fat fruit on the table
That one is an orange,
It looks so nice to eat
With its juicy insides and hard outsides
It's gotta be nice to eat.
Oh yes, that's a fat, stubby fruit on the table
That one is a lemon,
It doesn't look nice to eat
With its bitter insides and horrible outsides
It's gotta be horrible to eat.

Sebastian Batchelor (10)
St Olave's School

DOGS

D ogs are cuddly,
O nly when they're clean,
G reat house pets, but
S ome people don't like dogs.

A ngry sometimes,
R eady for anything
E nergetic creatures.

C ute and kind dogs are
U gly if they're bulldogs!
T ime consuming pets
E at everything they see.

Hannah Gilford (10)
St Olave's School

THE GOLDEN KEY OF TRUST

Trust is pure,
Trust is wonderful,
But only if it is used well.
If you trust someone,
You give them a key,
A golden key,
The golden key of trust.
They must keep it safe,
With all their heart and all their soul,
But if that person breaks the trust,
And the key is used,
Used for the room,
It unlocks the room full of dark, dark secrets,
They will escape stealthily and silently,
The golden key of trust will be gone,
And the trust will die.

Dominic Hanly (11)
St Olave's Shool

FRIENDSHIP

Friendship is a perfect thing.
It feels like pure luck.
It is a sort of love in its own strange way.

Friendship is a wonderful thing,
But if you throw it away,
You lose something inside,
Forever,
Like falling down a never-ending black hole.

Tom Scott (11)
St Olave's School

MY DOG

My dog is wild,
He jumps upon you,
And gives you a big kiss,
He is white and brown,
And paws everyone,
He would eat forever if he had the chance,
He's only a puppy really,
But he's huge,
He's strong enough to take you for a walk,
Instead of you taking him for a walk,
My dog is as fast as lightning,
And he's always ready to play with you,
He's an excellent footballer,
And he can pop any ball,
It's a challenge to keep the ball away from him,
He is cute and cuddly,
He runs around chewing his docked tail,
He follows me everywhere,
But the thing I like most is that he's my best friend.

Ben Eaves (11)
St Olave's School

THE BUILDERS!

Death to the builders,
Death to their vans,
Death to their beer cans,
Pants! Pants! Pants! . . .

Death to their noisy drills,
Death to their bills,
Death to their 'Hmm, this looks bad.'
Kill! Kill! Kill! . . .

Death to their scaffolding,
Death to their noise,
Death to their builders' bums,
Cry! Cry! Cry! . . .

Alexander Lee (10)
St Olave's School

CUP FINAL

We kicked off.
The fat forwards ran,
Crumbled the opposition.

The scrum half picked up the ball,
Spun it to the fly half,
How he chucked the ball I don't know,
But the winger caught it.

The crowd went wild,
As the fastest boy in Yorkshire,
Ran down the wing.

He handed off the fullback,
No one could stop him,
He was about to score.

Till their coach jumped on him,
And crunched his bones.
The whistle went,
The opposition were disqualified.
We won the cup.

Alastair Penty (11)
St Olave's School

Unusual Trees

Watch that tree,
It's bellowing at me,
With its brown trunk and green leaves,
It smells like a conker tree,
Maybe, it's a conker tree,
Its swinging branches here and there,
It's like it's windy up there,
Maybe it can see me.

'Hello tree' it stands there like a rock,
you can chuck something,
and it won't move a bit,
maybe it's a knight,
stuck as a tree,
with its grim face,
and wooden eyes,
maybe it might kill me,
with its green sword.

Callum Stark (10)
St Olave's School

Pleasure Is

Pleasure is having a weekend,
Pleasure is summer sun.
Pleasure is eating pizza,
Pleasure is having good fun.

Pleasure is playing football,
Pleasure is watching TV
Pleasure is having English,
Pleasure is being *me!*

Ben Naughton (10)
St Olave's School

THE CAT...

There once was a cat,
Who laid on his mat,
Not moving an inch,
Until the girl gave him a pinch,
He leapt in the air,
Thinking this isn't fair,
I only want to lie on my mat!

There once was a cat,
Who slept all day,
Until the children came to play,
With string and wool,
He joined in too,
Before he got bored,
And wanted something new!

Andrew Doyle (11)
St Olave's School

NEWCASTLE

N ever care if they lose
E verlasting goals from the opposition
W inning is not the point
C up matches are the same
A way or home matches, it doesn't matter
S ame old scores
T eams coming and going
L aughing at the team's performance
E verlasting shame.

Edward Mackenzie (11)
St Olave's School

WINES

Some wines are red,
Some wines are white,
It depends what sort you buy,
Some wines are bitter,
Some wines are sweet,
Come on have a try.

You could think some are sickly,
You could think some are nice,
You may have two glasses full,
Or you might have thrice,
You might want more and more,
But on the other hand you might want to go home and snore.

Edmund Pang (10)
St Olave's School

MY PUPPY NED

My puppy Ned is as cute
as a . . . cub!

My puppy Ned is as brave
as a . . . bear!

My puppy Ned is as sleek
as a . . . fox!

My puppy Ned is all these things
put together . . .
Guess what that is?
That is because my pup Ned is
the best dog in the universe!

Megan Hall (10)
St Olave's School

MY TEENAGE SISTER

It's my sister's 13th birthday,
She turned into an angry bull,
She complains,
Even when her plate is full!

Mood swings,
She starts to sing,
She sounds like a cat in a bag!

Black's her favourite colour now,
She drives us up the wall,
She's only happy,
When she's shopping at the mall!

But I live in my room,
A sink, TV and broom,
Will last me until I get *her* room!

Alice Jacobs (10)
St Olave's School

POEMS

Some poems are funny, they make you have a fit,
Some poems are sad and make you cry,
Some poems you can't make up your minds,
Some poems are boring,
Some poems don't rhyme,
Some poems describe, make people wonder why?
Some poems are silly, made up in time.
This poem is mixed up
So what type is mine?

Louise Walters (10)
St Olave's School

ELEPHANTS

Elephants are big and slow,
Not very fast can they go
With floppy ears and great big tusks
They amble slowly with little fuss
Their trunk swings to and fro
With legs like trees to make them go
A great big body, all rough and grey
And a stringy tail that won't get in the way
Tiny eyes like little black dots
And a wrinkly face that's been through a lot
They like to wallow in lots of mud
I'd like to be an elephant but it's not in my blood.

Oliver Hawking (11)
St Olave's School

FETCH BOY, FETCH!

'Fetch boy, fetch!'
My owner called at me.
'Fetch my kite,
in the conservatory!'

'Fetch boy, fetch!
My train's over there!'
'Fetch boy, fetch,
cos I really do care!'

'I know you're clever,
I know you're quick!
So please, please, please,
Bring back that stick!'

Anna Peach (10)
St Olave's School

WILD ANIMALS

Zebra stripes,
Giraffe spots,
Tiger lines,
Elephants' bots,
Monkeys' faces,
Rhinos' wrinkles,
Lion's roar,
Bear's paw,
Hippos sleep,
Kangaroos leap,
Birds tweet,
Cheetahs pounce,
Jungle leaves,
In the trees,
Of the big, big jungle.

Joy Barker (10)
St Olave's School

ANIMALS

Once there was a grizzly bear
Who loved to go to the fair
He was very funny
Because he didn't like honey
He only liked a pear.

Once there was an elephant that was very nice
He absolutely hated mice
When a mouse came near
He would run off with fear
Even if the mouse just wanted to share rice.

Jack Page (10)
St Olave's School

THE HOCKEY MATCH

We went to hockey
On a cold winter's day
We were so excited
Soon we will play
Dressed in red
We ran about
The whistle went
Everyone started to shout
The ball was hit
Will it go in?
Oh no the goalie's saved it
It's heading for that girl's shin
'Ohh' she screamed
She started to cry
We can't play anymore
We call it a tie.
We left the pitch
And drove away
When we got home
That was the end of the day.

Amelia Smalley (11)
St Olave's School

THE IMAGINARY CUPBOARD

A cupboard is a giant book;
the doors are the cover,
open them and it will lead you to an imaginary world.
It is a world of adventure and surprises
the only boundary is your own imagination,
it's the words of a story coming to life.

Christopher Dean (10)
Slingsby CP School

What Is A . . . Giraffe?

A giraffe is a long periscope, looking over plains,
Seeing scattering ants, looking for food.

A giraffe is a long ladder of brown and yellow paint
Reaching to long-lost sky.

A giraffe is a block of flats,
Towering under the sunlit Earth.

A giraffe is a giant horse chestnut tree,
With lots of animals on it.

Becky Swallow (10)
Slingsby CP School

A Kitten

A kitten is a miaowing furball,
It is a soft, fluffy furball rolling into walls,
It is a ball of fun,
A kitten is a bed all warm and cosy,
Keeping children safe in their dreams until
They wake in the morning,
A kitten is a fluffy teddy bear,
Which children cuddle at night,
Also thinking about it in the day.

Lucy Harrison (10)
Slingsby CP School

What Is . . . The Rainforest?

The rainforest is a plank of wood with many nails sticking out.
A wild zoo which encloses wild and endangered animals.
It is a giant field where animals' voices echo through the
    dense atmosphere.
It is a scaly snake which hisses as the sun disappears and the moon
    reappears as the night passes over the silent Earth.

Joshua Clarke (10)
Slingsby CP School

The Jungle

The jungle is a green multicoloured circus,
With different exciting exhibits.
There are tasty smells daring you to take a bite.
It is so warm you can almost taste the flickering air.
It feels like you're walking in imaginary air.

Emma Jane Hatfield (9)
Slingsby CP School

The Moon

The moon is a snoring sleepy face.
It is a nice good night feeling.
It is a tired bedtime story.
It is a full ball, growing in the sky night by night.

Lynsey Hatfield (8)
Slingsby CP School

WHAT IS A CLOUD?

A cloud is a soft, white bed equipped with covers and pillows
floating across the clear blue sky.
A bath of floating bubbles
tipping cold water on to the unsuspecting
people on the bustling Earth.
A face silhouetted in the sunlit sky.
A soft, fluffy cat playing with a big ball of wool.
A giant boat, sailing across the misty sky.

Rebecca Dring (10)
Slingsby CP School

THE MOLE

The mole is a worm-crunching beast which uses its razor sharp teeth to
munch on its lunch.
It is a blind giant, rumbling in its underground world.
It is a JCB digging at the saturated earth.
Its babies are big worms, blind and helpless -
But not for long!

Charles Morfoot (11)
Slingsby CP School

WHAT IS . . . A SHEEP?

A sheep is a cotton wool ball grazing in a field of daisies.
A sheep is a big ball of candyfloss waiting to be eaten.
A sheep is a fluffy ball of foam floating in the clear air.
A sheep is a Hoover, hoovering all the bits from the green carpet.

Natasha Pearse (10)
Slingsby CP School

THE UNPREDICTABLE UNIVERSE

One silly sun sweetly singing silly songs.
Two moody, messy moons making meteorites melt.
Three round, rolling rockets rocking ridiculously.
Four playful planets perfectly playing Pontoon.
Five constantly complaining comets crashing.
Six astonishing astronauts asking astro-belts for answers.
Seven sweetly smiling stars shining sensibly.
Eight blind black holes bouncing boisterously.
Nine nasty nebulas naughtily knocking nice neutron stars north.
Ten voyager spacecrafts venturing vaguely and visiting Venus.

Carrie-Anne Wallace (11)
Slingsby CP School

A SNAKE

A snake is a patterned shoelace,
wrapped tightly around its contracted, helpless prey,
patchwork patterns running down its back,
it opens its mouth bigger than a black hole.

A snake is a skeleton covered in quilted, patterned material,
its tongue is a flickering flame,
its body is a sleek car,
it frequently changes its attire and
is awarded some brand new garments.

James Baker (10)
Slingsby CP School

The Powerball Voyage

I am a powerball.
I come from the planet Mars.
I have come on a long voyage.
It is my revenge.
I was banished from Earth.
I have come to take over the world.
I am on the way to the centre of the Earth.
I am the most supreme one.
I have got all the power.
I have taken the world in my hands.
I am responsible for the world.
I am the god of all time.
I am the great creator.
I challenge the god to a battle.
I am going to win.
I would watch if I were you.

Danny Burke (10)
Stamford Bridge Primary School

Winter

Frosty cars in blankets.
Swirling snowflakes falling down.
Snow is crashing and falling.
Christmas is near.
Children throwing snowballs.
Children making snowmen.
Children playing in the snow.
Avalanches falling.
Ice cracking and crunching.
Getting stuck in snowdrifts.

Liam Archer (7)
Stamford Bridge Primary School

THE TIGER

I gently tiptoe through the leaves
That fall from yellow-orange trees,
Then I hear a sound
Across the leafy ground.
It sounds like a rustle
But
When I
Look again
Nothing moves a muscle.
Then something moves. Now I am sure.
I get irritated. I let out a roar!
I hear its footsteps running away,
So I chase after it. I want to slay
This creature who invades my space.
Why this very time or place
When I was having my rest?
I'll destroy him, little pest.
I lightly, slowly, steadily walk
Towards the bushes, eyes like a hawk.
Then it comes into sight.
A zebra with white
And black stripes on its back.
As I hide in the grass, my lips start to smack.
Now I duck down. I am very near.
At this stage I can very well hear
The animal's breath. It is gasping for air.
And now I dare
To bite at the food.
I am now in a hungry mood.

It lets out a yelp
As if calling for help
I drag it like a sack
Back
To my ravenous pack.
They all gather round, and soon it is gone.
And now my hunting work is done.
Yawning, I stretch down to bed
I am happy, for I am well fed.

Chloé Evans (10)
Stamford Bridge Primary School

DOWN MY STREET

As I walk down the street,
I wonder who I will meet,
It is a cold winter's morning,
On TV there was even a warning,
I am wearing my gloves, scarf and hat,
'There's my cat',
as I walk a bit more,
I look at the floor,
It is covered in snow,
'That was a windy blow,'
I walk over to the park,
'Was that a bark?'
I run to the slide,
'That was a good ride,'
I go to the swings and
Flap my wings.
And then I turn to walk home,
All alone.

George Dalby (10)
Stamford Bridge Primary School

SCARED!

It's dark,
and cold,
and wet.
As my feet hit the ground,
grass crumples beneath me.

A shadow creeps up behind me.

I carry on
and I think to myself,
it's cold,
and dark,
and wet.
I pass the swings slowly creaking,
in the icy cold wind.
A shiver runs down my spine.
The shadow still follows me.
Crunch, crack.
Dewdrops glisten in the moonlight.
The roundabout slowly turns.
The shadow still follows me.
The gate is in sight
a twig snaps behind me
I break out into a run
a gigantic stone looms ahead
I trip and fall
in the wet,
and cold,
and dark,
but I pick myself up
and carry on.
It is still cold
and dark,
and wet.

The shadow stops when I fall.
I turn around to find it is a
venom-spitting,
furry,
grey,
beady-eyed
monster!

I run for my life
but when I get to the gate
the monster jumps in front
of me in the
cold,
and wet,
and dark.
I scream
'Ahhh!'
The monster turns out to be
a tiny,
furry,
acorn-spitting
squirrel!

Emma Green (10)
Stamford Bridge Primary School

WINTER

Snowflakes falling, swirling, spinning,
Making snowmen from the snow,
Children sledging through the snowfall.
White is the beauty of the year,
Frozen puddles and sparkling lakes.
Ice is slippery because you can fall,
If a car slips it could end up in a ditch.

Roxanne Oldfield (7)
Stamford Bridge Primary School

AWAY FROM HOME

It's cold and wet, my feet ache
But I carry on running,
I can hear the sirens wailing, I can hear police, they're searching,
Searching for me.
I sit down leaning against a tree, thinking what it would be like at home
It would be warm and dry,
But Uncle Jim would shout at me, blame me,
I think I would be safer out here.
I can see a light looming,
Coming towards me, it's the police,
They're closer, it's clear.
I run as far away as I can, now I'm in the woods, no one's here
It seems like there is because the trees are blowing in the wind
Making it look like people are searching for me,
I'm scared!
I can now see intense coloured lights,
Creeping round the woods and wrapping up and strangling the trees,
I try and dodge them but they catch me,
I'm stood frozen there's no other way out of the woods.
Two policemen carry me out to the car,
I'm trying to guess what will happen next . . .

Sarah McLeod (10)
Stamford Bridge Primary School

A WINTER'S POEM

Winter is snowy and rainy
Misty and dull
Ice on the windowpane
Crispy snow on icy roads.

Glistening snow
Glistening icicles
Icy rivers
And snowy homes.

Chattering teeth
Noses red, lips sore
Snowy raw wind in your face
Snowflakes fall sparkling and crisp.

Thomas Smithson (8)
Stamford Bridge Primary School

IF I WENT TO THE MOON

If I went to the moon.
With spacesuit heavy
I would look back at the Earth.
The blue and green
Of the sea and ground,
I would look
At the world bigger than the moon
And think of my friends
Are they thinking about me?

If I went to the moon
With spacesuit heavy
I would walk as slow as a tortoise
The Earth's gravity would pull the moon around it
I would pick up rock and
Touch the dust with my gloves
Taking tests
Making footprints in the dust
I wish
I was on the moon
I wish,
I wish I was on the moon.

Rosie Burke (9)
Stamford Bridge Primary School

THE QUICK TRIP TO JUPITER

I went flying,
On my magic tricycle,
Faster than a motorcycle,
I touched the clouds,
I saw millions of crowds,
I landed on Jupiter,
And came back even stupider
Than I had been before,
My mum was mad,
I felt sad,
I wish I'd never been so bad.

It might have been quicker,
If I'd used a train,
Or even a plane,
Never mind I enjoyed it all the same!

Jonathan Andrew (8)
Stamford Bridge Primary School

WINTER

Winter is cold,
Hands raw,
Teeth chatter,
Rosy cheeks.
Accidents happen in winter,
Cars skid,
Some people go on icy lakes.
Snowballs made by children
Making snowmen is fun
Christmas is also in winter.

Sam Dalby (7)
Stamford Bridge Primary School

WINTER IS COLD

Winter is the time of year
When it is cold and frosty.

You get ice on the windowpanes,
You can feel the crunchy snow
Underneath your feet.

Noses are red and hands are raw.

In the snow it is freezing and cold.

But you can build a snowman in the snow.
You see hanging crystals in the sky.

And you get slush on the ground.

Lauren Cameron (8)
Stamford Bridge Primary School

IN THE AEROPLANE

In the sky I can see clouds rushing by,
I can see the crashing of the waves,
I can smell dinner on the aeroplanes.

On the second day I hear zooming jets,
I can see the tiny airport,
Where we are about to land.

Then I land at the airport,
Rushing to a taxi,
I see the beaming sunlight,
I am on my holiday.

Jack Winfield (8)
Stamford Bridge Primary School

WINTER IS

Winter is
Cold and frosty
Blankets of snow
Covering the ground
Icicles hanging
From windowpanes
A lacy filigree
Biting cold, our lips are sore
Hands raw, slush in gutters
Slippery roads
Icy puddles
My teeth chattering
Winds blow through streets
Laying a freezing carpet of snow
Runny eyes, nose red
I go in to sit near the fire.

Ryan Burns (8)
Stamford Bridge Primary School

MY SPECIAL JOURNEY

My horse took me through the countryside
On a wonderful journey I love
I feel the breezy air blowing through my hair
The flowers are swaying and I am saying
What a wonderful journey I love
Blue waters we spy, my horse and I
Set off at a gallop to reach the beach
And meet my friends where my journey ends.

Katie Agar (8)
Stamford Bridge Primary School

A SUMMER HOLIDAY

Summer is
Sunny and shiny, warm and hot
Going to the beach having fun
Making sandcastles, swimming in the sea
Having picnic getting sand in your sandwiches
Mums and dads sunbathing
Eating ice cream
Hoping it won't melt
Listening to the glistening sea
Jumping in the waves
Getting upset when it's time to go
Because you don't want to leave the beach
That was my summer holiday.

Emma Douglas (8)
Stamford Bridge Primary School

JOURNEY FROM EARTH

Tension mounting as the Earth goes miles, kilometres,
Millions of kilometres.
NASA said 'Go to bed for an hour or two.'

Mars and Jupiter big and then small.
Past solar systems, stars twinkle around you.
Gravity gets less and less,
As we go in the cosmos.
I see supernovas and planets,
Some big, some small,
In the cosmos.

Stuart Fraser (10)
Stamford Bridge Primary School

A Journey To The Office

There's not much happening,
Nothing at all,
Just trying to make my pen work
But there's no point at all.

Then suddenly everything changes,
And I spring from my seat!
I've been asked to take the register
So I try to look neat.

I walk up to the teacher's desk
And take it from the corner,
Then start to head for the door,
But then I trip right over.

I soon get up and head for the door,
Then drop a couple of things.
I bend over and pick them up
And fall over once more.

I haven't even got out the door
And have taken ten minutes already,
I brush my trousers off again
And now I'm definitely ready.

I walk out of the classroom,
And get to the office,
Drop the register on the desk,
Absolutely exhausted!

I'm glad I've eventually got there
But two dreads still remain.
The things they will say at break time
And the journey back to the dreaded classroom.

Hannah Warren (10)
Stamford Bridge Primary School

DIFFERENT COLOURS

Spring is
Flowers dancing in the sun
Pretty purple crocuses swaying softly
Red roses blowing in the breeze
White blossoms breathing softly
That is the colour of spring.

Summer is
Shiny, sunny, brightly yellow
Bright blue sky shining down
Splashing water from my paddling pool
I play with my friends in the sun
That is the colour of summer.

Autumn is
Brown, yellow, bronze and gold
Scrunchy leaves stamping on them
Leaves lying on the ground
I print leaves
That is the colour of autumn.

Winter is
White, brown, dull grey
Freezing cold, so cold
Snowy icy
Slush is on the road
That is the colour of winter.

Jessica Douglas (8)
Stamford Bridge Primary School

A TRIP THROUGH THE ROCKIES

I gaze through the tractor's windscreen
Across the steep mountainside
And see just the spot
The tractor comes lurching around some boulders
And chugs to a stop
At the push of a button
The boat slides slowly down its runners
To the cold water below
As I strap myself in
The water is gushing over the ledge
I pull a lever
And the boat is released
Suddenly I drop dangerously
And then lean scarily over some rapids
Then I winch myself in
And head for home.

Andrew Mathieson (8)
Stamford Bridge Primary School

WINTER

Winter is the beauty of the year,
It is really white and slushy too,
I love the snowflakes falling from the sky,
Fun is the best part of winter
To make snowballs play,
Winter can be very dangerous
Never go on ice!

Kerry Foster (7)
Stamford Bridge Primary School

I'M THE CAPTAIN ON THE DEEP BLUE SEA

I'm the captain on the deep blue sea
And I'm going to sail the seven seas.
Over the waves and under the moon
I'm going to sail them and sail them soon.

I'm going to sail them in my little boat.
It's small, red and wooden.
It's got a red and blue sail and a wooden seat to sit down
Two oars to row, up, down, up, down.

But suddenly a wave goes up
I feel like I'm going up.
Twisting waves and rain sprays around
Making me and my boat sink down.

I scream as a wave pulls us down
The water shoots at my face.
Then I grab the oars and drag us into calmer waters.

Claire Webb (8)
Stamford Bridge Primary School

WINTER

Winter is icy and slippery
It snows and snows as snowflakes fall,
Then the children play in the snow.
In the countryside people dress warm,
The cars go slow on the white blanket.
Trees are glistening in the misty dark night
Bare branches on trees fall off
Winter is icy and freezing
I like winter.

Sarah Stringer (8)
Stamford Bridge Primary School

A Voyage

On a walk through the rainforest,
On and on I go,
I hear the chat of some squabbling parrots,
Slithering snakes slide among bright green grass,
Monkeys swing from tree to tree,
Birds softly float in the blowing breeze,
Gorillas bash to and fro,
Tigers roar and scare the black and white monkeys,
Elephants spray water everywhere,
They stamp, stamp with joy.
My legs ache,
But still,
I walk on.

Rhea Goodman (8)
Stamford Bridge Primary School

I Imagine A Holiday

In spring
I imagine a boat trip.
This is what I see -
Dancing flowers in their rows,
Purple crocus and yellow daffodils.
This is what I hear -
Singing birds high in the sky,
The water swishing
From side to side
As the boat is sailing
Down the river.
I like spring!

Lucie Crowley (8)
Stamford Bridge Primary School

WINTER

In the winter
The snow makes a carpet
Across the paths and roads,
Icicles hanging like daggers,
From glistening trees
Bare branches and twigs,
In the winter
I see towns covered in snow,
Footprints up the paths.
A silent world of swirling snowflakes
In the winter
I feel the flurry of snow,
My chattering teeth
The chill in the air
In the winter.

Samuel Grice (8)
Stamford Bridge Primary School

WINTER IS THE BEST

In winter
The snow is deep
Cold blizzards
A fluffy carpet of snow
Trees glistening and freezing
On the river
Is sparkling ice
Winter is my favourite season
Winter is the best.

Michael Quinn (9)
Stamford Bridge Primary School

A JOURNEY THROUGH THE SNOW

Put on boots
Do up zip,
Open the door
And off we go!
Follow the footprints
To the pond,
Covered in ice
And round it we go!

Getting colder
Hands raw,
Jump over bush
And on we go!
Near the shed now
Getting closer,
Open the door
And in we go!
Get out the sledge
To go through the snow!

Hannah Dickinson (8)
Stamford Bridge Primary School

A MISTY WINTER

Sugar snow on my head,
Icy filigree all around me,
Crystal snowflakes where I tread,
Chattering teeth all I hear.

People wrapped up very, very warm,
People wearing fluffy and more fluffy coats,
But I'm warm and snug in my bed
Night! Night! Mummy.

A big yawn, ahhh!
People rushing to work already,
And they are wearing their fluffy coats,
Another morning of winter.

Trees frozen slant ways,
Rivers frozen stiff,
Fields with grass frozen up ways,
Houses with blankets of white on.

Amy Derbyshire (8)
Stamford Bridge Primary School

A VOYAGE TO NEPTUNE

2005.
We have landed -
We open the airlock -
We plant the flag.
Hooray!
I lay the first footprint -
I speak the first word.
I'm freezing
Very cold,
I need a very, very
Warm fire.
I take a sample of water.
I see the two moons,
I fall,
I stumble,
I rise,
It was good at the beginning and
Now it is dead.
It is like coming back from the
Dead.

Tom Wyles (9)
Stamford Bridge Primary School

A Trip To The Moon

One night I woke up in a fright
I found I was flying to the moon
On a magic vacuum cleaner
When I got there
Shooting stars were all around
The air was warm
The smell was horrible and fiery
There was not a sound
I don't think I like space any more
I got back on my vacuum cleaner
And went whizzing back home
I'm not going there again
No way!

Lauren Fletcher (8)
Stamford Bridge Primary School

Take Off Time . . .

3 . . . 2 . . . 1,
blast-off.
Like a thrown milk bottle,
Flames everywhere.
Slowly rising
Through the sky.
Shaking roughly,
Through the ozone layer,
Into the dark, black space,
With little twinkles here and there,
Orbiting Earth,
With a sweet, soft hum.

Samuel Happs (9)
Stamford Bridge Primary School

FLYING IN THE AIR

I zoom off into the air
Up and up and up.
I can see all the world.
Little tiny people in their cars.
Little tiny houses with little tiny trees.

Fluffy puffy clouds swirl around.
The dazzling bright sun shines in my eyes
The clear blue sky circling around
The twittering birds flying to and fro.

I feel the cold wind rushing past me.
I see the grass swaying down below me.
The sharp branches jagging about in the wind.
All the different colours of the rainbow.

Hannah Shaw (8)
Stamford Bridge Primary School

THE SEA WITH ME

Before I go on the journey I see a tree,
Near it is a pond I see,
I notice a jellyfish,
I make a little wish,
In my submarine I go down to the sea,
I am now under the sea,
The fish are beautiful nice little things,
I see a treasure box and ruby rings,
I meet a dolphin called Lee,
Under the sea.

Lauren Winfield (10)
Stamford Bridge Primary School

WINTERTIME

Winter is cold and wet!
Winter is freezing
Glistening icicles
Hanging from house roofs
Snowflakes falling
A soft, white blanket of snow
Children making snowmen
Playing on sledges
Having snowball fights
Chattering teeth everywhere
Sparkling ice on rivers
Seeing filigree on snowflakes
Glittering ice on the ground
Crystal cobwebs on trees.

Sean Cronin (8)
Stamford Bridge Primary School

TRAVELLING IN A SUBMARINE

Down, down, down to the bottom of the sea.
A submarine swimming what is that I see?
A great big dolphin looking at me
A great big whale swimming towards me
An angel fish swimming past.
A shark swimming fast.
He could be chasing me it's
Gone all dark I think it's time
To say goodbye, but wait -
What's this? An octopus
Pulling the shark off me.
Hooray! Hooray I'm safe at last
I better go, a few hours have passed.

Claire Swales (10)
Stamford Bridge Primary School

AN UNBELIEVABLE JOURNEY

Getting ready,
Excited, dreaming, thinking of what it'll be like,
A new holiday destination,
With palm trees and long, golden beaches,
Lakes and seas,
Pure,
Clean,
Aqua,
Open the airlock,
Get used to the bright light,
Disappointment,
Runs through my body as I look around,
Rocky,
Dry,
Dusty,
Dead,
Disappointment for the year 2004 voyage to Titan.

Sarah Epton (10)
Stamford Bridge Primary School

SPACE SHOT

And again the rocket goes up,
Once again it won't get any luck.
Up into space they now go,
All the people down below.
All the gas we're wasting now
All the chemicals whizzedy bizzedy
Pow!

Robert Palmer (9)
Stamford Bridge Primary School

SHOOTING TO SATURN

The engines are whirring,
The jets are blasting,
The voyager probe has taken off.
So many people with cameras and binoculars,
Taking pictures.
Drawing sketches of the probe,
I'm zooming past stars
And planets unknown
Earth is now a tiny microscopic dot,
Dodging comets and meteors, asteroids,
Jets burning.
Asteroids that was close!
I can now see our paradise planet.
The rings of Saturn,
Spinning like a car's wheel,
Landing of Saturn has come
Now for the moment of excitement
I place the English flag on the surface of Saturn,
Like an arrow piercing someone's heart.
Suddenly my eyes open,
What an amazing dream.
The first foot on Saturn.

Richard Cobbold (9)
Stamford Bridge Primary School

WINTER IS

Winter is cold and misty
Like an ice cube.
When you are outside
Noses are red
Lips are sore
Hands are raw
And eyes are runny.

The grass is covered in snow
White, soft and glistening,
Sparkling ice in the river.
Chilly and freezing
Bare branches and twigs,
A freezing carpet of snow
Then we build a snowman.

Jodi Townsend (8)
Stamford Bridge Primary School

A ROCKET SHOT TO SATURN

Whoosh!
The probe is whizzing through the air
Flying out of Earth's atmosphere,
Into the solar system.
Seeing the Earth so tiny,
Small and insignificant,
Just passing the moon,
Getting closer to Saturn.
With its rings of dust and debris
Captured by Saturn's gravity,
Bright colours circulating the air,
Then just passing Jupiter.
In five seconds we will land,
5, 4, 3, 2, 1 landing.
The airlock swings open,
Dead silence
I pick up a piece of moon rock,
It crumbles.
Suddenly I wake up,
Oh how real
Very exciting.

Danielle Gordon (9)
Stamford Bridge Primary School

THROUGH THE YEAR

Spring is
Dancing flowers in the sun,
Children giving them to everyone,
Yellow daffodils and purple crocuses
Peeping up through the new Earth
Newborn animals like lambs and calves
That is spring
Now is summer.

Summer is
Mornings are brighter and getting lighter
Nights are getting shorter and days are getting longer
Children laughing and having fun, in the garden
Dad's snoozing and Mum's sunbathing in the shade,
Going to the seaside and splashing in the sea,
And little toddlers playing in the sand,
That is summer
Now is autumn.

Autumn is
Rustling leaves on the trees
Children playing happily in the crunchy leaves,
Different colours red, yellow and orange
I love autumn
I love seeing the leaves fall gently down.
That is autumn
Now is winter.

Winter is
Soft snow landing gently on the glittering path,
Rivers freezing with ice on the blanket of white
Icicles on my garden gate freezing the rusty bars.
Winter is my favourite season.

Genevieve Wells (8)
Stamford Bridge Primary School

RELEASED

We've just been
Released by the rocket,
I'm shooting
Through space, approaching Titan
I'm nervous
Almost there
Turning down speed control.
Voyager has just come into orbit
Approaching Titan, Saturn's moon.
I can see some
Kind of liquid
Dark and black
I'm boarding the landing craft.
Excitedly approaching Titan's surface
Collect samples, souvenir
Rock for myself.
Water! It's definitely water
Samples.
Back to Voyager
Connected
Lift-off.
Return to Earth.
Take images of
Saturn's lovely rings
Titan's lakes and seas
Earth's gravity pulling me in
We're going to have a crash-landing
Boom.
That was an extremely lucky landing.

Elliot Newby (9)
Stamford Bridge Primary School

SPACE VOYAGE

Shooting through space,
A thousand miles per hour.
Sending images back to Earth,
Going through an asteroid belt,
Trying not to be hit,
Orbiting Venus.
Getting *very* hot,
Increasing speed to the moon,
Taking samples.
Moon rock, moon dust.
Making our way to Pluto.
Seeing all the colours of Saturn,
Red, orange and brown.
Viewing Saturn's 1000 rings.
Finally reaching Pluto,
Sending the first satellite pictures
Back through the solar system.

Richard Broadbent (9)
Stamford Bridge Primary School

MISSION TO ROCK CLIMBING

Up the stable, solid rocks,
Not a trace of any socks,
Lots of sweat running down,
With a horrible peculiar frown,
Lots of grip on your hands.
And your feet not on the ground,
Oh no I'm falling down,
I've just clung on with one hand,
Phew, I didn't touch the ground.

Martin Leadley (10)
Stamford Bridge Primary School

FIND A NEW PLANET

Finding a planet is hard,
But finding a new planet is harder.
Beating people to it,
Bashing them out the way.

Swerving past asteroids,
Dodging alien blasts,
And everyone's going berserk,
And crashing all over the place.

We're nearly there,
It's not so far.
A couple of light years away,
I can see it.
I think I might call it Planet Z.

Ruaraidh Whyte (9)
Stamford Bridge Primary School

UNDERWATER

Under the sea,
I can see.
Fish they're my favourite dish.
Crab I don't want to grab.
Jellyfish, mmm jelly.
The pressure is high.
I wonder why?
Oh no, I'll shoot to the sky!
Mayday, mayday,
This is the end of my day,
Whey hey!

Ben Grice (10)
Stamford Bridge Primary School

TITAN CRASH

Take off is commencing!
Moving through space,
Crew excited,
We see the colours and debris,
Of the planet Saturn.
It's like a giant sucked gobstopper.
Beautiful colours.
Amazing rings.
We zoom past Saturn,
Faster than I've ever been.
A moon's in view,
Almost ready to land on Titan.
This moon looks like Earth's moon,
With blood-red spots on its surface.
2004!
We're getting closer.
5 miles away,
From the dark, dead moon.
Its gravity isn't strong.
Only half a mile away
'All in landing positions!'
The captain shouts.
Crash,
Crush,
Our voyage ended with a
Disappointing
Crash-landing.
What will happen to us,
On the dead still,
Dead, dead, silent,
Soulless moon?

Alastair Wright (9)
Stamford Bridge Primary School

THE ENTRANCE OF THE DOOM STONE

The entrance looks spooky, very, very spooky,
Will we make it through? Will we make it through?
I hope we do, I hope we do.
Let's go through, let's go through.
Swish, swosh, swish, swosh.
What was that? What was that?
Arggh a bat! Arggh a bat!
We're running, running, we're running, running,
Oh no a lake, oh no a lake,
We'll have to make a raft, we'll have to make a raft,
Now we're going over, now we're going over,
Oh no a crocodile, oh no a crocodile.
Faster, faster, faster, faster.
Oh no a cave, oh no a cave,
In we go, in we go,
What's that? What's that?
Oh it's the Doom Stone, oh it's the Doom Stone.
I've picked it up, I've picked it up,
Oh no a monster, oh no a monster,
Now I'm going, now I'm going,
Over the river, over the river.
Now I'm running, now I'm running,
Past the bats, past the bats,
Outside the entrance, outside the entrance,
Into my rocket, into my rocket,
5, 4, 3, 2, 1 that's it folks, bye bye.

Robert Moore (10)
Stamford Bridge Primary School

A Mission To A New Planet

Going to a new planet
Nearly impossible,
Trying to land on it
Nearly impossible
1,108,526 miles away
Won't get there
With only 1,111,111,289
Gallons,
Will get there
Houston we have a problem,
Tanks burst, oil spilling
Going down at a mile a minute,
Crashed to the ground, didn't die.
Now everyone says goodbye,
We are off again on that
Impossible mission.

Andrew Hall (10)
Stamford Bridge Primary School

Walking On The Clouds

I imagined
I went walking
Floating in mid-air,
All soft and fluffy
Among the clouds.

I saw some magic birds,
And a golden apple tree.
A cold breeze blew in the clouds
And shook the little flowers.

I heard a train
Coming through a tunnel
In the clouds
To collect the tiny people on Earth.

Laura Baldwin (8)
Stamford Bridge Primary School

TAKE OFF TO TITAN

I have lift-off
I am excited
I hope everybody is proud of me.
I am going 100,000 miles per hour.
Orbiting the moon
Orbiting Mars
I am getting closer to Jupiter.
Am I getting lighter?
Getting closer and closer.
Getting tired,
Getting cold.
Then I see a planet
It is Saturn!
I am nearly there.
I get the first glance.
A dot
A boulder
A moon
It is Titan!
I am there.
The first person to get this far!
I wonder
Will I get back?

Michael Ward (9)
Stamford Bridge Primary School

MY JOURNEY TO MERCURY

M   y journey to Mercury is scary,
Y   ou should travel in a safe rocket.

J   ane, Rebecca, Katy and Sarah are with me,
O   ur other friends are at home,
U   gly aliens are attacking us,
R   ebecca kicked them out,
N   orman the driver made us crash,
E   ggs flew out to the rocket that we were racing
Y   es, we're nearly there.

T   here is Venus, it is in sight,
O   ver there Mercury must be.

M   ercury is in sight,
E   ggs fly out again,
R   eady to land,
C   rash!
U   gly aliens come to us,
R   ebecca kicked them out,
Y   ou stupid aliens!

Hannah Crowley (10)
Stamford Bridge Primary School

WINTER AFTERNOON

Snow is frosty
Cold and white.
Frozen lakes still and sparkly
And cold days.

Icicles hanging from window panes
Snow falling out of the sky.
A lacy filigree hangs from trees.
People frozen warming by the fire.

People playing in the snow
Children building a snowman.
Everybody chattering.
Sky is misty and dull.
It is going to snow again.

Lucy Glew (8)
Stamford Bridge Primary School

THE BIG MOMENT

Take-off!
To a dark spherical rock named The Moon.
Rumbling rocket sets on fire,
Leaving a silver tail behind.
Zoom!
Straight through Earth's atmosphere,
Into space goes the Eagle.
Into view comes the moon,
A beautiful view of Earth
Why did they call it Earth?
Why not ocean
As it is mostly water?

Two miles to go until we arrive at the dead, dark world,
Thump!
Apollo 11 has landed,
Out into the dark world the crew steps.
Silence!
Nothing to be heard,
Except for Neil Armstrong,
Saying the first word.
The first step has been taken.
This, is the big moment.

Jack Bond (9)
Stamford Bridge Primary School

In The Past

My mum's grandma, when she was younger
Worked in a mill
Helping to grind flour,
Now she is old, with hair that is white
And skin that is crinkled.

My dad is much younger
And likes to do magic
That is his job
He plays snooker with me.

When I am older I want to race motorbikes
I want to take the place of Edwards
Or Fogarty or Hager and enjoy my life
Racing motorbikes.

Charles Armstrong (8)
Stamford Bridge Primary School

Winter

Winter is cold and frosty.
Fog and gales.
Blizzards and snow storms.

Winter covers the countryside.
Rooftops in towns, fields and villages.

I feel happy in winter.
Inside by the fire.
But my hands are raw,
When I am outside.

Philip Main (8)
Stamford Bridge Primary School

NOW AND THEN

I step outside in the cold,
I see people young and old
A story is wriggling inside my head,
Like a book jumping to be read.

An old man, a very old man,
Did what he could and does what he can.
He wanted to fly up in the sky,
And tried his hardest not to cry.
He wanted to dance with the Sugar Plum Fairy,
And go to France on a big, blue ferry.
When he didn't know what to do,
He decided to invent computers and sticks of glue.
He was always out, never in,
He never believed in emptying the bin.
He wanted to wear a crown,
Never a frown.
You know those cards you get in packs?
He collected all the Jacks.
So there is a journey of life,
Now he only watches football,
The things he wished for never came true
Not one at all.

Life isn't something you can predict,
So while it is here enjoy it.

Olivia Alderson-Tuck (8)
Stamford Bridge Primary School

MY GRANDAD

There lived an old man,
My grandad.
His name is Harry
This is his life
It started like this . . .

Oh yes! Now I remember
He was once in the Air Force
Didn't fly them you know,
He just fixed them
To make them go.
All before I was born,
Flying, shooting.

But now he has retired
All gone, finished.
But he's still my grandad and always will be.
He's the only one,
The best grandad.

Matthew Fennell (9)
Stamford Bridge Primary School

MY FUTURE

When I grow up,
I'd like to be a footballer,
I'd like to play for Manchester United,
And be a professional.

I'd like to go to Wembley,
To score the golden goal.
And to play with Beckham,
Owen and Cole.

I'd like to sign autographs,
And be a little boy's hero.
I'd like to play in the Euros,
And to be on a video.

If they won't have me,
I'd like to be a bodyguard,
For my football hero,
(Michael Owen) If he's still around.

Adam Green (9)
Stamford Bridge Primary School

WHEN I LOOK IN THE MIRROR

I look in the mirror what do I see?
A smiling cute baby
Staring back at me.
I look in the mirror what do I see?
A pretty princess in a castle,
Being rescued by a handsome prince
That's what I see.
I look in the mirror what do I see?
An important, smart schoolgirl,
Staring back at me.
I look in the mirror what do I see?
A stressed teenager doing exams,
That's what I see.
I look in the mirror what do I see?
A caring mother working hard,
That's what I see.
I look in the mirror what do I see?
An old, wrinkle-faced gran
That's what I see.

Emma Doughty (9)
Stamford Bridge Primary School

My Grandad's Life

As a young lad bouncing out of bed,
It's a Saturday,
No school. Yeah!
Swimming day.

It's my ninth birthday,
Where's all my presents?
Ah, thanks!
That's the best so far,
A new football,
Can I go and play?

Oh, do I have to go to school?
Now I'm fifteen,
I don't care,
My birthday is boring!

Now I feel grown up,
Going out at night.
Meeting the girl,
Of my dreams.

Getting married,
In a beautiful church,
Buying our house,
Paying the bills.

All the children,
Having their turn.
Getting jobs, married too,
Having my grandchildren.

Better make the most of it,
Nearly time to go.
This will be the last pantomime for me,
I'm really pretty sure.

Charlotte Helme (9)
Stamford Bridge Primary School

A MISSION TO MARS

We have lift-off.
Faster than a stampede of elephants
Into orbit, on course.
Earth appears to float away
Silence,
Still,
Very strange.
What an astronaut has always dreamed of.
A mission to Mars.
A voyage of a lifetime.
Space, a still, dark world,
Mars is in sight,
Wait,
Increasing speed.
Going to land,
Spacesuit on.
Open the airlock
Red atmosphere all around
Samples of Mars
Rock, dust, liquids and gasses.
Back to the ship.
The craft had left Mars,
Mars is now an ant.

Ashley Patel (9)
Stamford Bridge Primary School

HER LIFE

The baby was crawling,
Crying and dribbling,

The schoolgirl was sighing,
Thinking and drawing.

The nurse with the needle,
Medicine and bandages.

The mother with the cradle,
Bottle and ball.

Then her funeral, the burial,
The sad end.

She liked her life,
Well . . . most of it.

Laura Hammond (8)
Stamford Bridge Primary School

ABOUT MY DAD

When he was young he lived on a farm,
He learned to use a gun,
And had lots of fun.

When he got older he got a job,
He was a cabinet maker,
And a very good one too!

Now he is older he is a caravan man,
He likes computers and PlayStations,
And he's a gas man too!

When he gets older he wants to have,
A new job
But he doesn't know what he'll be.

When he is very old,
All he will want to do
Is read.

James Ross (9)
Stamford Bridge Primary School

MY FUTURE

In the future I think I'll be
A new James Bond - that'll suit me.
With high-fly gadgets and spinning cars,
I might get a trip around Mars.

I might have guns and maybe bombs,
And I'll do stunts like Sean Connery ones!
I might see my hero - James,
Then we'll play some games.

Some other things that I'd like to do,
A trip to New York or Australia - they're alike
To get a big house, perhaps a mansion,
I could relax alone or help little children.

There is a hobby that I'd like to do,
Be a volcanologist - study volcanoes too!
I might change my mind, I'll tell you why,
If one erupts I might die.

I'll have a family, I'll tell you who,
I'll have two children - Max and Francesca,
I can't tell you who my wife will be,
It's top secret - the only one who knows is me!

Craig Benn (9)
Stamford Bridge Primary School

MY LIFE

When I was born,
I was crying like mad,
Until my mum picked me up,
Just before I was one,
I had my first little tooth,
Just when I was two,
I was picking up things,
Throwing them too,
When I was four,
I started nursery,
The best thing was my friends,
Now I'm at school,
Some of the lessons are fun,
And some are not.

George Leadley (9)
Stamford Bridge Primary School

HAMSTERS

A hamster lives in a cage.
He looks like a white, fluffy ball.
He moves slowly like a snowflake.
He goes for a run in his ball for ages.
Hamsters live in cages.
He gets out of his ball and climbs up his bars.
When tired he goes to his soft bed, to rest his sleepy head.
When he's awake he spins in his wheel
And then drinks from his cool shiny bottle.
When we get home his cage really stinks,
So I clean him out and he's very happy.

Ben Wynne (8)
Welburn CP School

THE SWAN

His sleek, white feathers
Are there to withstand all weathers.
His long, thin neck is for
Reaching out into deep water or
Reaching over to clean and preen himself.

And every now and then
With his bright orange beak
He would turn around and give
His pure white feathers
A nifty little tweak.

His soft, white feathers
As white as the whitest snow
And underneath he stands upon
Two large orange feet and on them he will go
Paddle, waddle, paddle O!

His huge white wings,
All outspread
As white as the purest white
He could be ready to fly away
Or coming into land instead.

Surrounded by a ring of cygnets
Or was it a cygnet-ring?
He would turn around and snap up some bread
That the humans would give
And to them he would bring.

Bethany Tildesley (10)
Welburn CP School

Our Naughty Jack

Our Jack scribbles on the wall.
Our Jack bounces with his ball.
Our Jack squeezes toothpaste on the dog.
Our Jack falls off a log.

Our Jack pulls my hair every day.
Our Jack screams for his own way (every day!)
Our Jack wakes me up early at five.
Our Jack wakes me up with a dive.

Our Jack messes about all the time.
Our Jack breaks things even mine.
Our Jack makes everyone cross including me.
Our Jack thinks he's the boss (but he's not!)

Our Jack climbs out of his car seat.
Our Jack is always untidy and never neat.
Messes my bedroom up every day.

Sometimes I wish he would just go away!
I love him really.

Amy Louise Batty (10)
Welburn CP School

The Lion

The lion is the king of the jungle,
He's proud and he's the leader,
He's a big meateater and he'll eat anything,
He sleeps all day but he occasionally gets up for a quick snack.

The lion is an expert hunter,
He runs swiftly and silently,
A flash of gold streaks after the gazelle,
The lion has caught its prey.

The lion cuts open the gazelle,
And starts to chew slowly,
When he has finished his dinner,
He goes back to his den, to sleep.

Nick Riley (11)
Welburn CP School

GIRLS

Girls fall out,
It's silly really, but mainly all about,
She did that, she said this.
That's my top.
Oh please stop!

Girls make up.
I mean they say sorry.
But all they are, are words.
I mean they're falling out by last break.
Oh for heaven's sake!

Girls what are they thinking?
It's a puzzle really.
One minute they're friends,
Then they're falling out by last break.
Little things like she wouldn't play with me.
Oh leave me out of it please.

But I'm happy when we make up
We're all friends for a while.
Tomorrow's another day though
What's going to happen I don't know.

Natalie Skirrow (10)
Welburn CP School

MY BROTHER

My brother
He's horrid to me
He picks fights with me
He blames everything on me.

My brother
He's nice to me
He takes me into town
He plays with me when I am bored.

My brother
He's the best
Even though he's horrid to me
But he looks out for me.

But now he's gone
Gone to live on his own
It's quiet now
Now I am on my own
I miss him!

Faith Somers (10)
Welburn CP School

THE CHEETAH

The cheetah lives in the jungle,
With other animals in the jungle.

He is spotty, big and thin.
He is brown like a tall tree.

He runs as fast as a train
And chases deer and tigers for his tea.

Nicholas Corbett (9)
Welburn CP School

HAMSTERS

Hamsters go to sleep in the day
Chew on bars at night.
Store their food at any time
And are noisy you know!
They look sweet in every way
They bite but it's ok!
Hamsters are many colours
Like brown, yellow, white and black.
Hamsters are fluffy like a pom-pom ball
And lively like children at home.
Hamsters sleep in the day.

Jessica Townley (8)
Welburn CP School

THE CHEETAH

The cheetah lives in the deep, dark, lonely jungle.
Its eyes burn like fire in the sun.

It has a golden spotted coat,
That shines in the sun.

It glides through the invisible wind,
And not a sound heard,
When the cheetah finds his prey.

However, beware because you may be
Next!

Ben Cohen (8)
Welburn CP School

SEA ANIMALS THAT I LIKE

I like dolphins
Swimming gracefully under the deep blue sea
Beautiful animals hunted nearly to extinction
Diving in and out of the Pacific Ocean
Skin is bluey grey.

I like clown fish
Scales are orange and white
Parting in and out of coral
They swim in many numbers
Eating coral and seaweed.

But most of all I like sharks
People think I'm mad because they think sharks eat humans
But they eat fish
They don't really harm humans
Sharks are one of God's creatures.

Katy Matthews (9)
Welburn CP School

MY HORSE PHOENIX

His coat is shiny and brown like a horse chestnut.
His black tail and mane blow in the breeze.
A white star twinkles from his forehead.
He tickles my cheek with his whiskery mouth.

Just like lightning he gallops around the field.
With his swishing tail following behind.
He glides like a plane over high fences.
Click, clack go his horseshoes across the concrete yard.

His powerful body can pull tractors from the mud.
Bucking back legs smash fences and poles.
Cows watch cautiously ready to move.
The bull trots away when Phoenix rears.

Patiently he waits for water, hay and mint bix.
Swishing his head over the stable door.
He never faces away when I talk to him.
Phoenix my horse, my best friend in the world.

Christopher Thorp (10)
Welburn CP School

MY DOG BEN

My dog Ben
He jumps up at me every day
He only thinks it's play.

My dog Ben
He knows when it's dinner time
Because he hears our own clock chime.

My dog Ben
He always has his own way
Because he barks all day.

The only way to calm him
Is to exercise him
Just like in a gym.
But it's good
When we play
With his ring all day.

Matthew Shaw (9)
Welburn CP School

MY MONSTERS OF BROTHERS

My brother Tom I think of him as a monster.
When we go shopping it's all cramped in the car
He takes it out on me.
It's always 'She's doing this and she's doing that',
He drives me round the bend,
I've had enough of this.

'Mum,' he shouts while I'm watching TV
I've said it once and I'll say it again,
He's driving me round the bend.
If you come to my house once I'm telling you,
You won't want to come again.

My brother Josh he screams all the time,
We get on well some of the time.
If Mum says 'He'll let you have a go when he's finished',
He'll say 'Mummy said you've got to let me have a go.'

When he hurt himself once I let him
Come to bed with me, and watch TV
When Mum came through to collect them to go downstairs
He recovered and ran down for breakfast.

Last of all there's Robbie,
He's a monster too,
He tips cherryade in his Pot Noodle,
He throws food all over the walls.

Lucy Holmes (10)
Welburn CP School

THE SHARK

The shark lies in a dark sea,
With lots of other animals.

The shark looks smooth on its black body.
Its teeth are sharp and pointed.

The shark moves its gills to breathe,
It moves its tail to swim quickly through the deep water.

The shark swims slowly to catch its prey.
When boats come near it scares them away,
With its sword-like fin.

You shouldn't mess with a shark,
As he will eat you up,
For a delicious snack.

Ben Daniels (8)
Welburn CP School